Reflections on the
Apostle
Paul's
Letters
to the Thessalonians

Devotional Readings in a Small Group Study Format

DR. RANDY L. JAMES

authorHOUSE

AuthorHouse™
1663 Liberty Drive
Bloomington, IN 47403
www.authorhouse.com
Phone: 833-262-8899

Published by AuthorHouse 03/06/2024

ISBN: 979-8-8230-2333-7 (sc)
ISBN: 979-8-8230-2332-0 (e)

Library of Congress Control Number: 2024904823

Print information available on the last page.

Any people depicted in stock imagery provided by Getty Images are models, and such images are being used for illustrative purposes only. Certain stock imagery © Getty Images.

This book is printed on acid-free paper.

Scripture quotations are taken from the Holy Bible, New International Version (NIV). Copyright 1973, 1978, 1984 by International Bible Society.

CONTENTS

Acknowledgements vii

Dedication ix

Forward xi

Introduction to First Thessalonians xiii

Chapter 1   The Beginning of the New Testament 1

Chapter 2   Real Success 10

Chapter 3   Discipleship in Action 22

Chapter 4   Living to Please God 28

Chapter 5   Times and Dates 39

Introduction to Second Thessalonians 53

Chapter 1   Greetings to the Saints 55

Chapter 2   Anchored in Reality 63

Chapter 3   How to Pray 73

ACKNOWLEDGEMENTS

Once again, I owe a great big "thank you" to my life's companion, Mary Jane James, who tirelessly proofread this manuscript and offered guidance for its' formating. She is my go-to person for the major needs of my life, and certainly the person whose critique I value most. If there are mistakes found in the printed copy of this book, they are mine and if so, they are probably there because I didn't heed something she asked me to include or delete. In any case, my wife is my treasure and I will always be in her debt.

DEDICATION

This book is dedicated to my grandson, Alexander Grayson James, with the hope and prayer that he will live out his life as selfless disciple of Jesus Christ. He is the beloved legacy who will carry on my name to the world beyond my years.

FORWARD

I n other books that I have written, I have tried to provide thoughtful commentary that would inspire the readers to meditate on the Word of God as daily nourishment for their lives. Though that is true for this book also, it has taken a form that is a bit different.

With so many churches going the route of small group Bible studies that provide interaction among those studying, it is hoped that these words and the questions that follow each section, will spur the Bible student to a deeper level of understanding. Some of the questions will bring about challenges for transformative change and some will create more questions that result from the ones listed. In either case, the prayer of my heart is that those who read these words, discuss them, and apply them to their lives will be richer in their walk with Christ as a result. As a minister of the Gospel that has been passed along to me, I could ask no more that this for those to whom the Spirit of God would speak during these pages of reflection.

INTRODUCTION TO FIRST THESSALONIANS

In order to best understand the letters of Paul to the Thessalonians, one needs to look at the background of how he came to interact with the people there. It would be of great help to stop and open the Bible to the book of Acts 17:1–15 and read about Paul and Silas' early days there.

Paul had entered into what is now present-day Europe due to a dream he had of a Macedonia man calling him to come and help them (Acts 16:6–10). He had originally planned go on eastward in his journey through Bithynia and most likely circle back to Antioch as he had done on his first missionary journey with Barnabas. However, Paul took this dream to be a message from the Lord, and he turned left instead of right as he opened new fields for the Gospel. We can only imagine what a different world it would have been if the gospel had been originally planted in Turkey, Georgia, and Russia, and parts of the world that are now heavily Moslem due to the heretical teachings of Mohammed. If that had been the case, the west might never have heard the Good News, or at least it would have been delayed for a long time. Thankfully, for whatever reason, we were blessed to receive the Gospel through our European ancestors.

In any case, once Paul pushed on toward the first steps of the evangelization of what is modern-day Europe, the city of Philippi was the inaugural soil for the testimony about Jesus to be planted. Paul and his companion, Silas, were put in prison for their ministry in the life of a slave girl, while Timothy, another companion, apparently was not arrested. The Lord worked through this experience, however, and by the time the disciples left the city, a church was established that was made up of one rich woman, Lydia, a slave girl, a jailer, and his family.

Because of their status as Roman citizens, who had been beaten and jailed without a trial, the local governing bodies treated the disciples well from the point of the discovery of their identities, but they were asked to leave the town. The disciples did so after meeting one more time with the fledgling congregation, then made their way toward Thessalonica.

All of this is background to the story of how God moved in a mysterious way to bring His light to the darkened areas of the world. In the same way, we need to aware of how the Lord may be working in our lives to help us share the Good News also. God has a great plan for our world and it is our privilege when we get to share in even a little part of it, for we never can get enough of the "Good News!"

There are five questions that need to be answered before we begin dealing with the specific contents of this first letter. First, "Why did Paul feel there was a need to start a church there?" Possibly it was chosen because he had a strategy to plant the gospel in such a vital place as a seaport to the Aegean Sea, and because it was a crossroad for a major land route as well. Though presently the area is contained within the country of Turkey, in Paul's time Turkey was made up of the provinces of Moesia, Illyricum, Macedonia, and Thrace. Thessalonica sat in the center of these land areas, and trade from far and near would pass through it. That means Paul planted the seed of Christ in a place where Christ's message would travel far beyond where he was able to take it personally. That's not a bad plan for church planting even today.

The second question is, "Who made up the church there?" Again, according to St. Luke's account in Acts, and from Paul's first letter to the Thessalonians itself, those who believed as a result of his ministry were truly an eclectic group.

"Some of the Jews were persuaded and joined Paul and Silas, as did a large number of God-fearing Greeks and not a few prominent women" (Acts 17:4).

"...for they themselves report what kind of reception you gave us. They tell how you turned to God from idols to serve the true and living God" (I Thessalonians 1:9).

A third question would be, "How long were Paul, Silas, and Timothy there?" We know that they were there for at least three weeks, but it may possibly have been a bit longer since Paul had time to work at his trade and built such a strong church that it bothered the Jews there greatly. Look at the following verses from Acts 17:2 and 17:5:

"As his custom was, Paul went into the synagogue, and on three Sabbath days he reasoned with them from the Scriptures."

"But the Jews were jealous; so they rounded up some bad characters from the marketplace, formed a mob and started a riot in the city. They rushed to Jason's house in search of Paul and Silas to bring them out to the crowd."

It most likely wasn't much longer than what is listed in scripture, however, because of the fierce persecution Paul faced there.

As we continue with our questions about Paul's ministry in Thessalonica, a fourth question that we need to ask is, "Why did Paul write such a letter?" Perhaps it was because he was there such a short time before being driven out, and because he was concerned about the welfare of the church in his absence. He eventually sent Timothy back to Thessalonica (3:1–3) from Athens to see how things were going there.

"So when we could stand it no longer, we thought it best to be left by ourselves in Athens. We sent Timothy, who is our brother and God's fellow worker in spreading the gospel of Christ, to strengthen and encourage you in the faith, so that no one would be unsettled by these trials. You know quite well that we were destined for them."

When Timothy returned with his report, Paul wrote this letter to affirm their success in the Lord and to strengthen them in their spiritual walk. He knew that new converts need instruction and training, and he wanted to supply what was missing in their faith.

"May he strengthen your hearts so that you will be blameless and holy in the presence of our God and Father when our Lord Jesus comes with all his holy ones" (I Thessalonians 3:13).

He also wrote to correct some misunderstandings concerning the second coming of the Lord, but we will deal with those particular passages in the coming days.

A fifth and last question that needs to be answered before we begin this study is, "From where and when did Paul write this letter?" Most likely it was written from Corinth after Timothy and Silas returned and reported about the progress of the church in Thessalonica to him. Paul had traveled to Berea, Athens, and finally Corinth after leaving Thessalonica (Acts 17:10–15). We know the date was around AD 50-52 because he was brought before Gallio, the governor of Corinth, during his time there (Acts 18:12–17). Paul stayed in Corinth a total of eighteen months, and ancient records show that a governor's term was only one to two years, and that Gallio began his administration there in the summer of AD 51. "So, Paul stayed for a year and a half, teaching them the word of God" (Acts 18:11).

We never know how God is going to direct the path of those who pledge themselves to His service, but we know that when the Lord is in it, fruit will be abundant in the long run.

Before we launch into the text of this letter, a few words more of introduction seem to be in order.

It all started off as what seemed like a good thing. Paul wanted to retrace the steps that he and Barnabas had taken on their first missionary journey in order to evaluate the progress of the churches they had planted. Just as they had done on the first trip, Barnabas wanted to bring along young John Mark as they ventured out. However, Paul and Barnabas disagreed on this because the first time around John Mark had left them midway in their journey, and Paul didn't want to provide another opportunity to the one who had let them down.

According to the biblical account, the discussion became so heated that the team decided to separate and each go their own way. At first glance it appears that this had all the earmarks of a carnal church split, but when one looks closer it can be seen that God had a plan which was being worked out even in this disagreement.

Paul decided to take another believer named Silas along with him and retrace the original route without Barnabas. Along the way he would complete his team by bringing a young man named Timothy into his group (Acts 16:1–5). Paul had most likely met Timothy on his first visit to Derbe, and when he crossed that place again, he saw something in the young man that caused him to believe Timothy was a valuable worker who needed to be enlisted in the Lord's work. Perhaps it was Timothy's family who had befriended Paul after he had been stoned and left for dead during the first journey (Acts 14:19–20).

After Paul decided to take Silas, Barnabas and John Mark sailed away to Cypress. We are not told more of their actions, but considering the character of Barnabas it would be safe to assume that they opened a work in Cypress just as Paul and Silas would continue to do in the north.

There are lessons here for us. First, we can see that God can use any circumstances for His glory—even what seems to be division and detours. It also shows us that Christians are not always going to agree on everything. Here is an example of two men who were filled with the Spirit of God, but couldn't find a common meeting ground. There is no disgrace in dividing the work of the Kingdom into different teams, or denominations. The only disgrace is when division causes a hindrance to the work of Christ.

An interesting sub-point that comes out of this continuing story is the fact that the Holy Spirit wouldn't let Paul into Asia and Bithynia (Acts 16:6–7).

We are not told why. We can only assume that God's plan for Paul and his mission was so specific that the course of history needed to be developed, and could only happen if Paul took a particular course in his ministry travels. In a night vision Paul was convinced that a Macedonian man was calling him in that direction, so he took this to be the leading of the Lord and turned to the west to continue on his journey.

Many questions could be asked of this story, such as:

1. Why would the Holy Spirit forbid Paul to speak the Word in Asia?
2. Does God ever tell us, "Not to" speak His Word to certain people or areas?
3. How does one know when "the Spirit of Jesus" does not allow us to do something?
4. Does God really have such specific plans that our daily moves can influence the course of history?
5. Does God use dreams or visions to let us know of His plans?
6. Could Paul have gone a different way if he had chosen to do so, or was he predestined to go west instead of east?

No doubt, many more questions could be raised, but answers to each will undoubtedly take serious discussion and consideration, which hopefully this book will compel.

What causes even more questions is the fact that Paul and Silas ended up going to jail for doing good (Acts 16:22–24). Again, on the surface it seems as if someone had either messed up or that the plan was off course in some way. However, apparently the only way to reach the jailer was to be in jail, and God allowed circumstances to unfold in such a way that this was possible. As a result, the jailer was converted, a church was planted, and the Philippian officials were humbled.

The story continued when another church was planted in Thessalonica and Paul was once again driven away (Acts 17:1–10). As a result of Paul's leaving Thessalonica, however, churches were planted in Berea, Athens, and Corinth (Acts 17:10–18:1).

The churches in Thessalonica were strengthened through letters, and we, as part of the Universal Church of Jesus Christ are still edified by Paul's letters to this day. Thanks be to God forever! Though man can't always see the outcome, God is always at work in our lives!

CHAPTER ONE

The Beginning of the New Testament

> **I Thessalonians 1:1–3** *Paul, Silas and Timothy, to the church of the Thessalonians in God the Father and the Lord Jesus Christ: Grace and peace to you. We always thank God for all of you, mentioning you in our prayers. We continually remember before our God and Father your work produced by faith, your labor prompted by love, and your endurance inspired by hope in our Lord Jesus Christ.*

As was mentioned earlier, this is a personal letter from the Apostle Paul and his companions, Silas and Timothy. As far as can be discerned, these words comprise the oldest surviving Christian writings, which make them very special indeed. In other words, though this letter is placed in the middle of the New Testament, according to the number of books contained therein, it is actually the beginning of the New Testament, for it is thought to be older by at least a decade than any of the Gospel accounts or other letters (Mark was written in approximately AD 65 and I Thessalonians most likely around AD 52).

From the first verse, where Paul spoke of the Thessalonian Church as being "in God the Father and the Lord Jesus Christ," one gets the impression that he wanted this young congregation to realize that it gets its breath, strength, and purpose solely from the Lord. Certainly, Paul was thankful for the church and had some very nice things to say about it, for he wanted them to know that in his prayers he daily commended this congregation to their heavenly Father.

So, what made these new Christians the kind of people to be remembered and cause Paul to be thankful? It was because of their work that came about as a result of their faith. The letter to the Hebrews tells us, "Now faith is being sure of what we hope for and certain of what we do not see" (Hebrews 11:1). They had, by faith, come to experience a relationship with God, and that relationship translated in to action in His name. These baby Christians had become new creatures and their lives had been radically changed since hearing the message of the cross.

Faith is at the heart of everything we do and say when it comes to our Christian walk. We are saved by faith, we are sanctified wholly by faith, our baptism is an outward expression of the new life we have received by faith, and communion is accepted as a sacrament of grace by faith. We may not have all the answers for this world, but we walk by faith trusting that when it is all finished, our faith in Christ will be rewarded.

QUESTIONS FOR DISCUSSION

1. Can you say that your church is truly "in God the Father and the Lord Jesus Christ? Why, or why not?
2. What things can you thank God for when you think about your church?
3. Can you see, with eyes of faith, beyond the problems of your church, to things that are praiseworthy?
4. What do you think it was that transformed these baby Christians into mature saints of the faith?

Faith—Love—Hope

I Thessalonians 1:3 *We continually remember before our God and Father your work produced by faith, your labor prompted by love, and your endurance inspired by hope in our Lord Jesus Christ.*

Paul was also thankful that their labor was prompted by love. People may work for a paycheck, or they may work out of a fear of losing their jobs if they don't stay at their assigned tasks, but people who work because they are in love with what they do will never be unemployed. People contented with, or excited about their work, don't keep an eye on the time clock or count down the years until they can retire, because the task that employs them energizes them as well. Such was what Paul saw in these Thessalonian Christians. Apparently, he had witnessed this dedication when he was with them and continued to give God praise on their behalf for such an example of diligence.

He was equally grateful to God because these people were able to endure whatever the enemy of their souls could throw at them because they had been inspired by the hope that is only found in Christ. There was the hope of the resurrection, the hope of Christ's constant companionship through the presence of His Holy Spirit, and the hope of accomplishing the mission of grace that had been entrusted to them that kept them on their assignment even when the going got tough. The Apostle himself had to sneak out of town under the cover of darkness (Acts 17:10), but these faithful disciples continued to live out their faith publicly and with boldness. No wonder Paul received such great satisfaction and joy because of the report that had been brought to him by Timothy. Here was the greatest gift that any spiritual father could receive; the church he planted was being effective for Christ.

Anyone who has ever been a part of a church plant knows exactly what the apostle was feeling. As a pastor who has pastored various sized church over the years and has been a part of starting a church from scratch, it is a wonderful thing when I get news that one of my previous charges is doing well. Ministers resign and leave churches for different reasons, but every place of service holds a special spot forever in his or her heart. Each church has been prayed over, preached to, taught in the Word, and built over time. When one has been a part of baptizing believers, dedicating babies, receiving new members, and burying the saints, there is a part of oneness forever. May the people of God always know that they are loved and prayed over.

QUESTIONS FOR DISCUSSION

1. Paul uses the trio of "faith," "love," and "hope" to describe the church in Thessalonica. What effect did this trio accomplish to benefit the church?
2. How is your local church alike or not alike the church Paul describes?
3. Do you think endurance was the result of their faith and love, or could it be attributed to something else?
4. Do you think the church is stronger by going through the adversity of not having a pastoral leader in place, or was their progress due to other factors?

> **I Thessalonians 1:4–5** *For we know, brothers loved by God, that he has chosen you, because our gospel came to you not simply with words, but also with power, with the Holy Spirit and with deep conviction. You know how we lived among you for your sake.*

One claim that the Apostle Paul made to the church is that the gospel he declared was more than just words. It was power that came from the highest source, from the presence of God Himself. Because God had poured out His power on them, He also had chosen them for the task of using that power to save the world. This is the kind of predestination that is truly biblical and echoes Romans 8:29, where Paul wrote to the church of how it is God's plan that all men should be conformed to the image of His Son. God desires it for us, but He does not force us into that kind of relationship. He is powerful enough to give us free will without being threatened in His sovereignty.

There was a conviction among Paul's team as to their mission. They had a job to do and there was no time to waste. It's a good lesson for Christians of all generations to understand, namely, if one doesn't believe in what he or she is doing, he or she might as well not do it.

There was also a deep conviction on the hearers from the Holy Spirit. What do we mean by conviction? Conviction is the strong impulse that comes upon a person that helps us determine the rightness or wrongness of an issue. What is the difference between Holy Spirit conviction and general Christian convictions? The Holy Spirit speaks specifically, and general convictions can be based on one's interpretation of scripture, or perhaps have been formed by one's culture.

Throughout my years in the church, I have many times heard someone say that they had particular convictions about doing or not doing certain things. Sometimes it had to do with Sabbath observance, modesty in dress preferences, whether or not the length of one's hair is a spiritual matter, or even whether or not it is proper conduct to eat or drink in the church. The list is endless when we try to consider what is right or wrong for Christian living.

What Paul was referencing here was an anointing from the Holy Spirit that comes with power and evidence of God's presence. The gospel was presented with intensity and that power changed lives. This is more than ones' preference or culture. God's conviction goes to the heart—always!

QUESTIONS FOR DISCUSSION

1. What does Paul mean when he said, "the gospel came to you not simply with words?

2. What power is Paul talking about? What does that kind of power look like?

3. How do we recognize the Holy Spirit's power among us?

4. What is the difference between having convictions and being under conviction of the Holy Spirit?

The Highest Form of Flattery

I Thessalonians 1:6 *You became imitators of us and of the Lord; in spite of severe suffering, you welcomed the message with the joy given by the Holy Spirit.*

Just as children often follow the pattern of their parents in the physical sense, so also the child of God usually follows the lifestyle and practices of his or her spiritual parent. In the case of the Thessalonian church, they lived as Paul lived. He was only with them for a short time, but in those few weeks Paul resided among them in such a way as to establish a blueprint for holy living.

He also noted that they experienced what Christ did. This included severe suffering, for it has always been and will always be that where the suffering is the greatest, the church grows the strongest. From the earliest days of Christianity to the present time, this truth remains, as was related to me by a selfless church planter in South Sudan when he said, "Where there is no shedding of blood, the church doesn't grow."

This is where the present-day Christian in the Western world has to ask the question, "Do we really want that?" Churches that have gotten used to their padded seats, air conditioning, central heat, stage lighting, technical prowess, and money for expensive programing, many times do not approach Christianity with the full acceptance of a cross for every Christian. One has to wonder if Jesus would not have included the self-satisfied church in His rebuke to Simon Peter in Matthew 16:23 when he said, "Get behind me Satan! You are a stumbling block to me; you do not have in mind the things of God, but the things of men."

They also welcomed the message of the Holy Spirit. Apparently, they were open to new truth and change. When Paul opened the way for them to receive the Spirit and taught them to sense His leading, they were eager to move forward in the ways of God.

The sad truth is that many people never make it that far. Far too many who have endorsed the name of Christ relate more to things of the world than they do the ways of the Spirit. If we hear and follow society's siren calls rather than the still small voice of God, we are in trouble. When we listen to what social media proclaims above what the Word of God declares, we are on dangerous ground. In times like these, it is time to take a lesson from this ancient church and follow the ways of the Lord instead the choices of pleasing ourselves.

QUESTIONS FOR DISCUSSION

1. Who stands out as a role model of the Christian faith to you?
2. How have you imitated that role model in your faith walk?
3. Is the moving of the Spirit in our midst always accompanied with suffering?
4. How can we have joy in the midst of our suffering?

Faith is the Victory

I Thessalonians 1:7–8a *And so you became a model to all the believers in Macedonia and Achaia. The Lord's message rang out from you not only in Macedonia and Achaia— your faith in God has become known everywhere.*

Who are the role models in your life? Would it be your mother or father? Would it be a teacher, professor, coach, or community figure? Would it be a political stateman, a civic leader, or some military man?

How we answer that question tells a lot about our priorities in life and what our own reflection might be to those who are watching us. I can think of three men who had a big impact on my life. One was a scout master, who after long days in the factory took time to train young men in the areas of camping, hiking, tying knots, and woodlore. Another was a high school running coach who mentored me significantly in the sports of Cross Country and Track. I will always be grateful to these two men who knew how to motivate me to do more than I could ever do solo.

However, the one person that I looked to most for my life's path was the pastor who shepherded me through high school. Though he was only in my community for five years, his friendship and encouragement in my ministerial endeavors stayed with me for decades after that.

Paul reflected on how the Christians at Thessalonica had a huge impact on their peers. Throughout the regions of Macedonia and Achaia their reputation spread, but according to these words their testimony for Christ went even far beyond those provinces.

What was it that was becoming known? It wasn't their fancy building, because they didn't have any. It wasn't their choir or style of music that made an impact. It wasn't even their great numbers, because they were a young and struggling congregation. What made a different that others could see was their faith in God.

It was their faith in God that caused the Lord's message to ring through their vicinity. It was their faith in God that held them fast when the days of persecution bore down heavily on them. It was their faith in God that would keep them through the lonely hours, the working hours, and periods of joy. We may try many things to impact our world, but it is our faith that wins the victory. Role models come and go in our lives, but a faithful witness for Christ makes a difference for eternity.

QUESTIONS FOR DISCUSSION

1. What's the difference between being a role model of the believers and a role model for the believers?
2. How far has the work of God in your church moved beyond the church walls?
3. Are we being the kind of example now that generations of Christians to come will talk about? How?
4. What is the key that makes Christianity a subject to be talked about in the community where a church is planted?

Serving the Living Lord

I Thessalonians 1:8b–10 Therefore we do not need to say anything about it, for they themselves report what kind of reception you gave us. They tell how you turned to God from idols to serve the living and true God, and to wait for his Son from heaven, whom he raised from the dead—Jesus, who rescues us from the coming wrath.

The word got out to others about the Thessalonian Christian's faith in Christ. Whether or not our faith is truly transformational tells on us too—and that can be a good thing or a bad thing—depending our relationship.

We find that they turned from their idols. Paul found them in demonism, astrology, and in multiple pagan temples. Mount Olympus was only fifty miles away, and that place was the hotbed of paganism and idol worship. In order for the Christian in Thessalonica to remain strong in the midst of a pagan world they had to make sure there was no compromising their faith in God.

Here is another lesson for the church of the twenty-first century. Whatever becomes our highest priority is our idol. Whether it is self-rule, apathy, our own goodness, or our own comfort and pleasures, there can only be one Lord. When baseball or football games keep Christians from the house of God on Sundays, this is a yielding to the pagan ways of a godless society. When our free time or families take so much of our schedules that we don't take time to pray, study the Word, or be involved in ministry for Christ's sake, then those things have become our idols and we have ceased to be examples of the resurrected Christ. When the activities of children set the schedule for families, we are in trouble.

Paul wrote that they served the true God. They had joy in the Holy Spirit, for they had become followers of Christ, part of the team, and a growing witness to the glory of God. They had found a commitment and contentment in Christ in spite of the great pressures from non-believers.

They also looked for Jesus to return. Many saints never expect to die, but with the biblical exceptions of Enoch (Genesis 5:24) and Elijah (II Kings 2:11), they all have so far. So here are some lessons for us:

1. Be prepared for Christ's coming. Be ready at all times.
2. Be anticipating His coming. Expect Him at all times.

3. Be liberated through Christ's coming. Break free from sin's bonds and ties.

Such is the example this ancient church proclaims to our church today.

QUESTIONS FOR DISCUSSION

1. How does our faith "get out?"
2. What tangible results can be seen because of our faith in Christ?
3. What do we consider to be our highest priority?
4. Does thinking about the coming of the Lord bring us joy or dread?

CHAPTER TWO

Real Success

I Thessalonians 2:1–2 *You know, brothers, that our visit to you was not a failure. We had previously suffered and had been insulted in Philippi, as you know, but with the help of our God we dared to tell you his gospel in spite of strong opposition.*

Sometimes it's hard to discern between what is success and what is failure. In many ways it looked like what Paul was doing lacked the blessing of God, for ever since he entered into Macedonia he had been running into obstacles.

First there was the imprisonment in Philippi, then his team was run out of town in Thessalonica. When they got to Berea there was some initial success, but then they were driven out of town again. In Athens Paul had mixed results, and in Corinth he was worried that his overall labors might have been in vain. It's true. Sometimes in the present sense we can't really tell whether we are winning or losing.

Of course, we have the luxury of looking back on these pages of history and would heartily agree that the Apostle was a trailblazer for the gospel, and that his foundational work would be built upon by countless others. After all, he isn't considered to be "St. Paul" for nothing.

Throughout our days we may also sometimes wonder if we are being productive for the Lord, or are just marking time. I know of many pastors who ask that question on a regular basis as they preach sermon after sermon on Sundays, attend to the sick, feed the poor, encourage the downhearted, and take on many other various duties. Does anyone really get changed by all that we do? Is there success that comes from our daily labors?

Whether we are a part of the clergy or the laity, we need to remember that no cup of cold water given in the name of Jesus will ever lose its reward (Matthew 10:42). We may work in a factory, in a department store, serve fast food, or teach in a classroom, but every act of kindness and blessing has an impact that goes far beyond our ability to grade. Our Lord is watching over our every move, and He knows our heart and intention even if it isn't apparent to others.

Paul no doubt got discouraged at times, just like us, but be of good cheer! Jesus has already won the victory and He will bless the work we do in His name. You can take that to the bank!

QUESTIONS FOR DISCUSSION

1. How do you define success in ministerial endeavors? Why?
2. How do you define failure? Why?
3. How do we encourage ministers who are dealing with depression?
4. What tangible steps can we take, in Jesus' name, to live out our discipleship before the world?

Sincere Concern

I Thessalonians 2:3–4 *For the appeal we make does not spring from error or impure motives, nor are we trying to trick you. On the contrary, we speak as men approved by God to be entrusted with the gospel. We are not trying to please men but God, who tests our hearts.*

Every year our colleges and universities give out honorary doctoral degrees. One has to wonder if it wouldn't be more appropriate for Christian colleges and universities to give out honorary nursing degrees, signifying the care giving side of ministry rather than the administrative focus of a doctorate. Most likely, Paul would have thought such to be appropriate.

To love the church as Christ did means that we must care as Christ did and put our caring into practical action. From the outside world in both Philippi and Thessalonica, Paul's character had been under attack. Some charged him with theological errors, having impure motives, and using trickery. However, his response rebuked such attacks, as he simply said, "I care."

As a mother cares for her children, and this is revealed in the fact that he endured patiently (vs. 2), he was able to bear the insults and rage of his enemies. No doubt he recalled the pains he had endured at Philippi just before he traveled to Thessalonica, for it had not been an easy experience for he and

Silas to be imprisoned, whipped, and put in the stocks, but he was able to bear much for the cause of Christ.

He was also able to bear the weaknesses and imperfections of his converts. He had just been able to be with them in Thessalonica for approximately three weeks, so they no doubt took many missteps along their spiritual journey, but he gave of himself sacrificially to them. Satan's traps against the people of God in all places, throughout all generations, are temptations for self-promotion, self-gain, and self-glory. However, Paul took on this job for the Lord, seeking no pay and seeking no glory for anyone but Christ.

There will no doubt be times when people will accuse us of doing what we do from selfish motives. But if we are genuinely serving our Lord with a pure heart, we can know that like Paul, we can proclaim our innocence in such matters. What really counts if that God is glorified by what we do and say, for then spiritual fruit will come from our efforts in some way eventually. So let people talk; the truth will someday shine like the sun.

QUESTIONS FOR DISCUSSION

1. Is it ever right to use trickery to bring people to Jesus? Does the end justify the means if a person's salvation is at stake?
2. Is an "honorary nursing" degree for ministers more appropriate than an "honorary doctorate?"
3. What is a Christian response to attacks on our personal character?
4. How do we best overcome focusing on "self" instead of "servanthood?"

Glorifying God

I Thessalonians 2:5–6a *You know we never used flattery, nor did we put on a mask to cover up greed—God is our witness. We were not looking for praise from men, not from you or anyone else.*

Paul loved enough to share the gospel. The word "gospel" means "good news!" He did this even through strong opposition, for this was more than a job to him because like many present-day pastors in many parts of the world, he received no salary. He shared the message of Christ out of a love for God and man.

Paul also loved enough to share his life. No one can share the gospel without sharing a part of his or her own life. As the old saying goes, "People don't care how much you know until they know how much you care." Therefore, we must win the right to share the "Good News." People come to church the first time for many different reasons, but usually they will only return if they have found a human connection there. The siren songs of the world without Christ calls out to everyone who shows even the slightest inclinations toward spiritual matters, but when the people of God follow Paul's example and genuinely become a conduit for God to pour out His love, then Christianity becomes more than just a religion.

Because of his great love for the Lord and for people, he never did anything for selfish gain. He had no idea that someday people would revere him as "St. Paul," or name churches, hospitals, and schools after him. These things had to have been the farthest things from his mind, for he was involved in the lives of people for the glory of God and the salvation of souls. He didn't do it because he just thought it was a good idea; he did what he did because he felt the thumb of God in his back driving him forward to cover new ground for the Kingdom of God.

It's so easy for us to get caught up in the value systems of this world and try to achieve things that look good in the eyes of men. We build huge cathedrals, massive campuses, outstanding ministries that cater to thousands of people, and often think that we are accomplishing much by doing so. Certainly, there is nothing wrong with bigness, but if what we build is not of God then it is built for nothing. If we are just building a name for ourselves, our denomination, or our particular ministry, then we have left the spirit of God's plan, and the Holy Spirit will not bless us. Our task is to work as Paul did, selflessly and diligently for the glory of God, not to glorify ourselves.

QUESTIONS FOR DISCUSSION

1. How does the church's value system and the world's value system differ?
2. How do we "win the right" to share the Good News?
3. Does God still put "His thumb in the back" of His called servants? How would we know?
4. Is bigger better, or is bigger just bigger?

I Thessalonians 2:6b–9 *As apostles of Christ we could have been a burden to you, but we were gentle among you, like a mother caring for her little children. We loved you so much that we were delighted to share with you not only the gospel of God but our lives as well, because you had become so dear to us. Surely you remember, brothers, our toil and hardship; we worked night and day in order not to be a burden to anyone while we preached the gospel of God to you.*

Perhaps one of the greatest needs of society next to the gospel, is the development of a strong work ethic. Paul gave such an example, for he labored consistently. We need to be about the business of "supporting our habit," which is sharing the gospel, with our diligent work. We are to be good stewards of our time and we are to be godly craftsmen.

Paul labored so that he would not be a burden and he believed in each person pulling his or her own load. In the church we are each to do our fair share. This includes tithing, visiting those who are needy, discipling the believers, praying for the lost, teaching righteousness, and continuing in the path of holy learning. We need to be living examples for Christ in the way that offers others something to testify about concerning us. As important as it is that we would always have a testimony to share concerning what Christ has done and is doing in our lives, it is equally important that we have such a reputation that others can talk about to the glory of God. That's when our life truly becomes a witness, for what we do speaks much louder than what we say.

The truth of the matter is that we can destroy our Christian testimony and witness with one quick rash action. We may be faithful in many areas of our life to the cause of holiness, but if we don't govern our words, our attitude, and our knee-jerk reactions, onlookers may be turned off and turned away from a personal faith in Christ themselves. Certainly, we would never want to be guilty of keeping someone from coming to faith or stumbling in their walk.

As Paul did, we must always remember that our church is part of Christ's Church. We bear His name, so we need to look and act the part. Perhaps we should put out a sign on the marquees of our church that reads, "Help Wanted: Christian Nurses." That might give our Christian colleges and universities something to think about. It's very possible that the Apostle Paul would have been proud of the idea.

QUESTIONS FOR DISCUSSION

1. What does a Christian work ethic look like?
2. Can a Christian ever do his or her "fair share?" How is it measured?
3. In what way can our Christian witness be destroyed?
4. If we are Christian, do we reflect Christ—in—us?

You Are Witnesses!

I Thessalonians 2:10 *You are witnesses, and so is God, of how holy, righteous and blameless we were among you who believed.*

Every brand-new parent soon realizes that there is more to parenting that just having kids. Parents also realize very quickly that the time entrusted for each child in the areas of guidance and training is very limited. Even though we may have nearly twenty years to help our young find the correct path for his or her life, rare is the father or mother who feels that they have been given sufficient time to effectively teach all the life-lessons that need to be learned.

This was the problem Paul faced with this church, but he had a much smaller time-frame in which to work. How does one raise up a spiritual family in less than a month? No wonder he waited with concern for Timothy to return with a report on the welfare of this baby congregation.

If we want our children to turn out in a way that would be pleasing to God then we need to follow Paul's parenting policies. Previously, Paul considered his actions toward the church to be like those of a nursing mother, but now he defines himself as taking a father's role.

Our example is so much more important than our advice. The odds are that the spiritually young will become no more spiritual than the role models whom they emulate. This why a Christian example requires purity. The psalmist asked and answered his own question, "How can a young man keep his way pure? By living according to your word" (Psalm 119:9). To live this life, we need the sanctifying grace of God.

A Christian example also requires integrity. Honesty, fairness, and dependability are the characteristics that separate those who walk with Christ and those who are self-serving.

A Christian example requires blamelessness. This is not "sinlessness," or "mistakelessness," but a walk before the Lord that is innocent of any willful rebellion. We will never reach a point of perfection in this world where we are not capable of sin or not being guilty of human error due to body frailty or the exercising of poor judgment at times. However, we can be blameless in the sense that our hearts have been purified in motive by the love of God, and the very nature of sin can be removed from us. We can be an outflow of holiness because of the Spirit that fills us, and that is what Paul was referring to in this letter.

QUESTIONS FOR DISCUSSION

1. As people are witnessing your life, what would you like them to see?
2. Is there a parallel between raising children and bringing up spiritual infants? In what way?
3. What is the difference between being faultless and being blameless?
4. Can a person ever really be free from sin?

Living Worthy of the Lord

I Thessalonians 2:11–12 *You are witnesses, and so is God, of how holy, righteous and blameless we were among you who believed. For you know that we dealt with each of you as a father deals with his own children, encouraging, comforting and urging you to live lives worthy of God, who calls you into his kingdom and glory.*

There are so many things that can discourage people. One doesn't have to look too far to begin making a "depression list" whereby people can lose heart because of their circumstances in life. Paul reminds this church that he wasn't like that. He was about the business of encouragement as they began their walk with the Lord. He did this by speaking words of comfort. One can almost hear his reassurance to this young congregation, "You're going to make it! We're behind you all the way!" Providing cheer is a good practice for Christians, for parents, and even for spouses. The world often beats people down, but a few kind words can lift them up again.

Paul also encouraged the believers by speaking words of instruction. A charge was given here as he said, you have been "urged" and "called." Direction, discipline, and warning are all advices that are needed at one time or another. We need to learn to measure when to apply each one.

When Paul said that we are to "Live lives worthy of God," we acknowledge that it's a tall order. He didn't mince any words or lower the bar for new believers just because they might have it rough where they are. He points to the fact that this goal is for all. Then and now, this is not just a standard for preachers, but for all who would be a part of the body of Christ. It is also true that this goal requires all from us. There is no way that Christians can serve the Lord half-heartedly and meet the standard of holiness that God expects from His people, for this describes the life of total submission. Just getting by is not enough.

One more thing that we see here is that this goal promises all that we need. God calls us into His Kingdom and glory. We have so much more to gain than we could ever lose when we follow fully after Christ.

We remember that Paul only had approximately three weeks to live such an example before the church in Thessalonica. Most of us have a much tougher job, for we are called to minister where we are planted—and that calling may be for a lifetime. Only one foundation will make our spiritual journey finish on the right note, and that foundation is Jesus.

QUESTIONS FOR DISCUSSION

1. How do we encourage people in their walk with the Lord?
2. How do we apply direction, discipline, and warning without being judgmental and overbearing?
3. Is it right for a Christian to feel unworthy of God's love?
4. Is there a difference in what is required of the clergy and the laity when it comes to Christian living and witness? Explain.

Reasons for Thanksgiving

I Thessalonians 2:13 *And we also thank God continually because, when you received the word of God, which you heard from us, you accepted it not as the word of men, but as it actually is, the word of God, which is at work in you who believe.*

Earlier Paul thanked God for the Thessalonians because of three things (1:2). He was grateful for:

1. Their work produced by faith.
2. Their labor prompted by love.
3. Their endurance inspired by hope.

The interlude from 1:2 through 2:12 has been a description of Paul's ministry. Basically, he had been talking to the church about the example he had set for them, the love he had for them, and the plan God had for them. These were words meant to encourage their hearts and keep them headed in the right direction.

At this point Paul said that he also thanks God continually for the Thessalonian church because they received the Word of God. They didn't consider it as coming from men. From the account given to us in Acts 17, we find that they influenced some Jews, a large number of God-fearing Greeks, and several prominent women. These people accepted God's Word as God's Word, not some watered-down ideology produced by Paul or some leaders in Jerusalem.

It was no doubt thrilling for Paul to see that the words he spoke about God was steadily at work in the believer's lives. Perhaps it would be beneficial at this point to question why many people today don't take the truth of God as sincerely as this example of a baby church, which is given to us from the first century A.D. We could ask, "If it's God Word, then why don't we retain more of its truth?"

Perhaps we need to look not only to the church as an institution, but also to the home. Home is where Christian nurturing happens or doesn't happen in the lives of believers. Each generation needs to pass on the faith to the next generation so that the latest one can see that this is something that stands the test of time and doesn't pass like a fad. It's easy to point our fingers at the group that meets weekly, but in reality, it's what happens in the homes of our congregations that tells the story of whether the faith will be real or just a ritual. God's Word is God's Word for all generations.

QUESTIONS FOR DISCUSSION

1. For what reasons can you give thanks for your church family?
2. When we study the Bible, how do we keep the main thing the main thing?

3. How does Christian nurturing at church and Christian nurturing at home differ?

4. How is God's Word at work within us?

Suffering for Jesus

I Thessalonians 2:14–16 *For you brothers, became imitators of God's churches in Judea, which are in Christ Jesus: You suffered from your own countrymen the same things those churches suffered from the Jews, who killed the Lord Jesus and the prophets and also drove us out. They displease God and are hostile to all men in their effort to keep us from speaking to the Gentiles so that they may be saved. In this way they always heap up their sins to the limit. The wrath of God has come upon them at last.*

These words paint the picture that Judean Christians knew much about suffering. They suffered from their own countrymen, and they suffered for the same reason as their brothers, for in Judea the Christians suffered persecution from those who killed Jesus and the prophets. These who opposed the Gospel of Christ in Thessalonica also did their best to drive believers away from the faith.

The Thessalonians, like the Judea Christians, faced people that displeased the God of love by trying to keep folks from the truth through their violent acts. Paul assured this baby congregation that the sins of such agitators were piling up, and God has already determined their fate.

So, what do we learn from this? First, we need to remember whose word the truth is and feed on it. This way we can be sure that the Father is pleased with our actions and we ourselves will be better equipped to face the hardships that will inevitably come our way from time to time.

We also need to realize that suffering can be from the Lord, and though it may be unpleasant, it can be a good thing. Without imprisonment, it is unlikely that John Bunyan would have written *Pilgrim's Progress*. Without her imprisonment in a Nazi concentration camp, we probably would never have heard the testimony and witnessed the ministry of Corrie Ten Boom. Without a life of poverty among the lepers in India, it is doubtful that Mother Teresa would have won the Noble Peace Prize and become a household name. Suffering and hardship go hand in hand for those who are called to take up their cross and follow Jesus. Even a seed must go into the ground and die before it can spring up to new life.

Our heavenly Father is in charge, and He will have the final say at the end of the day. We don't have to worry as to whether or not He is keeping score. If the sparrows can't fall without His knowledge and the flowers of the field can't bloom without His care, we are sure He can take care of us.

QUESTIONS FOR DISCUSSION

1. What does being an imitator of God's church look like?
2. How is suffering and the Christian experience linked?
3. Is it possible to be a Christian without suffering?
4. Can you explain "feeding" on the Word of God.

Separation Anxiety

I Thessalonians 2:17–20 But brothers, when we were torn away from you for a short time (in person, not in thought), out of our intense longing we made every effort to see you. For we wanted to come to you—certainly I, Paul did, again and again—but Satan stopped us. For what is our hope, our joy, or the crown in which we will glory in the presence of our Lord Jesus when he comes? Is it not you? Indeed, you are our glory and joy.

It's a common thing for families to experience many anxious moments when they are first separated. Whether it's the first day a child goes off to camp, the first day at school, or the first night away from family, there is often a sense of foreboding or withdrawal pains concerning those we love.

Paul was experiencing such feelings of withdrawal from his spiritual family. What many people do not understand is that the church is more than a business to a shepherd of the flock. The spiritual, physical, emotional, and financial welfare of his or her people truly becomes the focal point of pastoral living. Paul had only spent three weeks with the people of this church and he had to be wondering how things were going. Since the time he had departed that particular flock, he had been to Berea, Athens, and Corinth, but he continually must have wondered how the people of Thessalonica were doing.

Therefore, he sent Timothy and Silas from Athens to find out, and he waited for their news.

The reason Paul was so concerned about this congregation is because he believed that the enemy of their souls, the deceiver and murderer, Satan, was out to destroy them. Though there are many people today who downplay the role or even the existence of the evil one, Paul didn't take him for granted. The Prince of the Air, though defeated at the cross, still has his hooks in those who don't put their trust in Christ to deliver them from his influence, so Paul was anxious as to how those young Christians were handling his traps and schemes.

Though Satan had no control over Paul, or over we who trust Jesus for our salvation, we all are still afflicted by the presence of evil in the world. It is not God's will that people should suffer, that they should kill each other, that graft, greed, slander, and bigotry should exist in society, but as long as the enemy is still on the prowl, the spell he casts over his dominion still attempts to thwart the plans of God. Satan will ultimately lose and the Kingdom of God will rule forever, but for a time we should all be wary and wise when dealing with the forces of darkness.

QUESTIONS FOR DISCUSSION

1. How does Satan stop a Christian like Paul?
2. Does a Christian go through withdrawal when they are separated from their church family? How?
3. Is it fair to say that Satan is still out to destroy God's people?
4. How was Satan defeated at the cross, yet still active against God's mission today?

CHAPTER THREE

Discipleship in Action

---

*I Thessalonians 3:1–3 So when we could stand it no longer,
we thought it best to be left by ourselves in Athens. We
sent Timothy, who is our brother and God's fellow worker in
spreading the gospel of Christ, to strengthen and encourage
you in your faith, so that no one would be unsettled by these
trials. You know quite well that we were destined for them.*

Athens is one of the oldest cities in the world, with some people speculating that it was first inhabited as early as 5,000 B.C. By the time Paul arrived there it was a place that was full of idols and paganism was rampant. It was also a place of higher learning, a place of great need, as well as a place of great wealth, according to Acts 17. Paul did his best to cross the cultural bridge to minister to the inhabitants there.

He had to work alone, however, for he had sent Timothy on a mission to build up the people of Thessalonica, who had been facing persecution because of their new-found faith in Christ. Though it's not mentioned specifically in this passage, most likely Silas went along with Timothy since Paul spoke of being alone. Such solo ministry times were rare for Paul, but necessary under the circumstances.

When I was in the early days of my ministerial training, one of my professors used to say, "Every Timothy needs a Paul and every Paul needs a Timothy." Over the years I have found the wisdom of this statement, for a number of reasons. First, there is safety in numbers. There is also the blessing of encouragement when one doesn't have to minister alone. However, one of the strongest reasons for having a mentor-mentee relationship is because on the job training is the most effective type of discipleship.

Every generation has a responsibility to share the gospel with the next generation, otherwise the work of the Kingdom would die out. It's good training for the senior worker to learn how to impact the life of the junior and good role modeling for the junior to glean from the senior. The work is too important to be left to chance.

The question then, that each of us need to consider is, "Who is discipling us," and "Who are we discipling?" Paul knew that hard times would eventually come for every soldier of the cross and only through disciplined training could he prepare Timothy for it. If we haven't found one to train, we need to, for the Lord is counting on us as surely as He was on Paul.

QUESTIONS FOR DISCUSSION

1. Are there times when "solo" work for Jesus is necessary, or is it more effective and scriptural to work as a team?
2. How would you define the concept of "discipling?"
3. What are the benefits of being a disciple-maker?
4. What are the benefits of being discipled?

What's Happening?

I **Thessalonians 3:4–5** *In fact, when we were with you, we kept telling you that we would be persecuted. And it turned out that way, as you well know. For this reason, when I could stand it no longer, I sent to find out about your faith. I was afraid that in some way the tempter might have tempted you and our efforts might have been useless.*

Because of the way Paul had to leave Thessalonica (Acts 17), it's reasonable for him to have been concerned about the physical well-being of this congregation. He could have wondered if they literally would have been able to survive, because many saints have died for the faith in Christ they professed. However, the apostle's main concern here seems to be spiritual, not physical. First, he was concerned that they had truly received a new life in Christ. He knew that true transformation is not just an emotional high or even a social acceptance produced by spiritual entrapment. A new birth is just that—an experience of being truly born again by the Spirit of God.

He was also concerned that the new life would be making them effective for Jesus. Paul sent Timothy and Silas to get answers to some questions. It's most likely that he wanted to know how he was faring. Since we are saved from our sins in order that we may be salt and light to the world, being productive and effective for the Lord is the real evidence of real change.

No doubt he was concerned that their life in Christ had not died out. Had time weakened their commitment to the faith? Had temptation and trials from the enemy won out? Had inactivity led to a slow spiritual death? From the words of the text, Paul was somewhat desperate to find out.

Few people who are not clergy will ever realize the time that is taken up by prayer, and the consuming focus that is involved by a pastor for his or her flock. Paul set the example for us because Jesus set the example for him. As they prayed for the welfare of their people before the Lord, it is important that each shepherd remembers that prayer over a congregation is just as much a part of ministry as preaching to them. One is done publicly and the other privately, but both are essential for spiritual growth.

QUESTIONS FOR DISCUSSION

1. What is Christ doing in you?
2. What are you doing for Christ?
3. How is your new life affecting the world around you?
4. How is your prayer life affecting you?

Good News at Last!

I Thessalonians 3:6–9 But Timothy has just now come to us from you and has brought good news about your faith and love. He has told us that you always have pleasant memories of us and that you long to see us, just as we also long to see you. Therefore, brothers, in all our distress and persecution we were encouraged about you because of your faith. For now we really live, since you are standing firm in the Lord. How can we thank God enough for you in return for all the joy we have in the presence of our God because of you?

There was no doubt a great sense of relief and joy when Timothy returned and gave Paul the news that he had been waiting to hear. There was a blessed three-fold message that Timothy delivered.

First, Timothy gave a report of an active faith. III John 1:4 says, "I have no greater joy than to hear that my children walk in truth." Apparently, Paul felt that way too. Good pastors always rejoice when his or her congregation or a former congregation gives evidence of a living relationship with Christ.

Timothy also gave a report of Christian love. Pastors rejoice when their church members have a relationship with each other. Christians who can't get along with each other are a source of grief to their own communities and lead a miserable existence as well.

Timothy gave a report of harmony between Paul and the people of the congregation. Pastors again rejoice when they hear that their people have warm feelings toward them. The congregation is the pastor's life and nothing gives the spiritual leader, in this case, the Apostle Paul, more joy than to know that his spiritual children were standing firm in the Lord.

If harmony in the church body produces such joy among the believers, it is certainly something that every church should strive to achieve. The sad thing is that some congregations are ever striving to reach such oneness, but never seem quite get there. However, there are steps to take to make it happen.

It begins by repenting of wrong doing and humbling ourselves to one another. It continues in prayer as we lift up friends and foes alike for the Lord to deal with as He sees fit. As we plead for the Holy Spirit to refill our lives with His love, we listen for His voice to guide us in any steps we need to take to bring about unity. Harmony is possible when God's people pray.

QUESTIONS FOR DISCUSSION

1. What kind of impact do you think your spiritual life has on your pastor?
2. Does your church exhibit the presence of love, or is it a source of grief?
3. What would it take to make your congregation overflow with joy?
4. What are the steps it would take to get there?

Increasing and Overflowing Love

I Thessalonians 3:10–13 *Night and day we pray most earnestly that we may see you again and supply what is lacking in your faith. Now may our God and Father himself and our Lord Jesus clear the way for us to come to you. May the Lord make your love increase and overflow for each other and for everyone else, just as ours does for you. May he strengthen your hearts so that you will be blameless and holy in the presence of our God and Father when our Lord Jesus comes with all his holy ones.*

These verses are filled with lot of things for us to consider. Verse ten tells us that Paul desired to supply what was lacking in the faith of the congregational members in Thessalonica. The New English Bible renders the same verse, "to mend your faith where it falls short." Moffit's translation says, "...to supply what is defective in your faith," and William Barclay translated these words as, "...to fill up the gap in your faith." Obviously, Paul had something serious in mind as he would speak to the King of kings on their behalf.

He offered prayers for the increase of their love. He knew that spiritual growth was vital. It means getting beyond the emotional—not "falling in love" the way some would fall off a ladder. It means experiencing the fullness of the love of Christ.

He offered prayers for the development of an inner strength. This is so these new Christians would have power to endure persecutions and power to live abundantly. There are always traps from the enemy of our souls, so we need to develop a strong enough connection with Jesus to be overcomers to all the obstacles the devil puts in our paths.

He offered prayers for them to be living blamelessly when Jesus returns. There is a need for spiritual cleansing and there is joy when one knows that he or she is clean. Complete forgiveness of sins is available for everyone who calls on the name of the Lord, and complete cleansing from the nature and power of sin is also available. This is why Paul prays that they would be blameless, not faultless, when the Lord comes again.

Paul inferred that these people were his friends and his life. The church is not just a shepherd's job; it is the shepherd's family. The calling of ministry is not what one is hired to do; it is what one is called to do. Paul needed his followers to know that he was concerned about them, wanted to have joy in them, and that he was praying for them. That, in short, is what a shepherd's life is all about.

QUESTIONS FOR DISCUSSION

1. Is there an area in your life where your spiritual connection to Jesus seems to fall short?
2. How do Christian develop an inner strength?
3. What's the difference between being blameless and being sinless?
4. How would you describe a pastor's "call" from God?

CHAPTER FOUR

Living to Please God

I Thessalonians 4:1–3 *Finally brothers, we instructed you how to live in order to please God, as in fact you are living. Now we ask you and urge you in the Lord Jesus to do this more and more. For you know the instructions we gave you by the authority of the Lord Jesus.*

This is one of the most important passages for the church, whether in Paul's day or in ours. No doubt the Christians in Thessalonica were trying to live to please God already, but Paul pressed them to do so even more. The question is, "What do we do to please God more?" The answer is that we are to live holy lives before God. That prompts a second question, namely, "How exactly do we do that?" Here the Word of God in the following verses give us some specific insights.

We begin with the importance of knowing the instructions that have been given to us, the qualifying of the importance is found in the authority that comes with those instructions, and the authority for them is found in the person of Jesus Christ.

There is no way for us to stress strongly enough the power that is found in the name of Jesus and the authority that comes along with that power. It doesn't matter what society says, what social media says, what our government says, or even what our family says, for the Christian is to always take his or her cue for living from the person of Jesus Christ. If we can't agree on that then we really can't believe anything the Bible has to say.

It is made it very clear in Matthew 28:18, "Then Jesus came to them and said, 'All authority in heaven and on earth has been given to me.'" I don't see any way that these words should leave any doubt as to who needs to be in charge of our lives.

So, if knowing the instructions given to us is so vital, then we need to become deep consumers of the Bible, the written Word of God provided to us. This is the primary source for information and guidance for all who would become Christ followers. It means we need to read it, remember it, and follow it as we make our plans, because after all, though it was not written directly to us, it definitely was written for us.

Why do this? Because we are making it our primary mission in life to live to please God. The church in Thessalonica gives us our example and Paul commends them for doing so. Who are we to do anything less?

QUESTIONS FOR DISCUSSION

1. What does living to please God mean to you?
2. What are some tangible ways you can show your faith?
3. How do we gain instructions from God?
4. How do we honor the Bible without idolizing it?

It is God's Will that We be Sexually Pure

> **I Thessalonians 4:4–6** It is God's will that you should be sanctified; that each of you should learn to control his own body in a way that is holy and honorable, not in passionate lust like the heathen, who do not know God; and that in this matter no one should wrong his brother or take advantage of him. The Lord will punish men for all such sins, as we have already told you and warned you.

I've developed a practice over the years, of highlighting, underlining, and scribbling notes in my Bible when I find specific words, phrases, and ideas that strike home to me personally, so when I read, "This is God's will for you..." I sit up and take notice.

Often people inquire, "How can I know God's will for my life?" Well, this one of those places where we shouldn't have any question, for Paul makes it perfectly clear for us. We are to be holy; we are to be sanctified if we wish to live to please God.

The very idea of sanctification is debated by people of various denominations as to when it happens, how it happens, and to what degree it happens. Certainly, it's a topic on which honest people can disagree and discuss at length. However, Paul doesn't give us any wiggle room when it comes to understanding what he means in this context. In this place, being sanctified means being pure sexually.

If we ever needed a message to be proclaimed from our pulpits (for those churches who still use pulpits) or in the public arenas of the twenty-first century, it is this. If Christians are going to live to please God, they must live free from the sins of fornication, adultery, homosexual acts, and all like works of darkness.

This is not a popular message, for society has come to the point where its sexual practices are like alley cats, but our day is not so different from the temptations faced by the church in Thessalonica. In an immoral world, Christians are to stand out like light and influence society like salt. If we are like the world without Christ in this regard, we have become people who no longer desire to live to please God, for this is His will for us.

This means, if you are married—stay married, and stop looking around for other options. If you are single—stay sexually pure and abstain from promiscuous behavior. If you are addicted to porn, then confess your sin and seek help and counseling from your Christian family. If you are tempted to homosexual behavior, resist, live celibately, and trust God for grace to free you. We are the people of God, so let's live like it!

QUESTIONS FOR DISCUSSION

1. How can we know God's will for our lives?
2. Does being in control of our own bodies lead to sanctification?
3. Does sexual immorality disqualify us from salvation?
4. How does being sexually pure honor God?

Sanctity Through Surrender

I Thessalonians 4:7–8 *For God did not call us to be impure, but to live a holy life. Therefore, he who rejects this instruction does not reject man but God, who gives you his Holy Spirit.*

Paul made it clear that wronging our brother (or sister) by participating in sexual connection with them, cheapens them. Our brothers and sisters are people, not objects to be used, for being used is degrading. We can't undo the damage later because memories die hard, and guilt feelings can cling to us even when we are forgiven. The consequences for sexual sin can be severe and can include disease, pregnancy, pain, and the breakdown of one's marriage. If we wrong our brother or sister then we risk eternal destruction for ourselves and them, for we are violating a person for whom Christ died.

The answer to impurity is purity, and the pathway to purity is a holy life. We are to belong completely to God through the sanctified life, a way that is possible only through the cleansing and keeping power of God through His Holy Spirit.

Naturally, people don't want their sexuality taken away, for it is a gift from God to us to be used in the context of marriage. However, for us to live to please God, this desire must be controlled, for self-control is one part of the fruit of the Spirit (Galatians 5:22–23). Self-control comes with the filling of the Spirit. Being Spirit filled will keep us holy before God and will lead us to be conformed to His will. Being Spirit filled also keeps us holy before men and helps us build a strong character and reputation.

The pathway to the sanctified life that Paul calls the church to is found by surrendering all that we are, all that we have, and all that we will ever have, into the loving hands of Jesus. He is able to not only forgive us for the acts of sin we have committed, but also able to cleanse us from the nature of inbred sin that caused us to do what we did. As Paul writes later on in this letter, "May God himself, the God of peace, sanctify you through and through. May your whole spirit, soul and body be kept blameless at the coming of our Lord Jesus Christ. The one who calls you is faithful and he will do it" (5:23–24). We will deal with this more when we get to the last chapter of this letter, for the need for holiness cannot be over emphasized.

If any believer rejects these instructions, it's the same as rejecting God. The Father will never deny Himself or be inconsistent with His Word, and there is no room for situation ethics in His Kingdom. These commands are given to us on the authority of Jesus Himself, who gave us His Holy Spirit to make our obedience possible.

QUESTIONS FOR DISCUSSION

1. How would you define "impurity" before God?
2. Does having sex outside of marriage cheapen our partner?
3. How do the gifts of the Spirit enter into the sexual relations discussion?
4. Does the reception of the Holy Spirit exempt us from sexual temptation?

Love, Real Love

> **I Thessalonians 4:9-10** *Now about brotherly love we do not need to write to you, for you yourselves have been taught by God to love each other. And in fact, you do love all the brothers throughout Macedonia. Yet we urge you, brothers, to do so more and more.*

This would be an appropriate scripture for Valentine's Day, as Paul spoke of love in the context of the first part of the chapter, namely, the evidence of living a holy life. There was no separating the spiritual and secular life in Paul's thinking, because we are brothers and sisters in Christ always, or not at all.

Love must be a divine institution, for it is commanded and exampled by Jesus. "This is my command: Love each other" (John 15:17). "A new command I give you; Love one another. As I have loved you, so you must love one another" (John 13:34). "My command is this: Love each other as I have loved you" (John 15:12).

The idea of brotherly love comes from the Greek word, "phileo." This is the love one has for another person in a family relational way (brother, sister, mother, father, etc.). However, the idea of being "taught by God to love" is another matter altogether. The word for love here is "agape," also from the Greek language, but where the source of love is found completely in God the Father. Agape love is the evidence of the new birth in Jesus Christ. It's true, though, that where "agape" abounds, "phileo" will also abound. A love from God will also produce a love for people, and certainly there was mutual concern for the brothers during the times of persecution when the church at Thessalonica was established (Acts 16–17).

We must also understand that love must be practically lived out (vs. 10). This passage is a perfect example of Acts 1:8. The church is to witness love to people like themselves (Jerusalem/Church), it is to witness love to people who were similar to themselves (Judea and Samaria/family, friends, neighbors), and they are to witness love to people different from themselves (the ends of the earth/the whole world without Christ).

Finally, love must be continually increasing. Have you noticed how we keep trying to "grow" the church all the time? We never seem satisfied with what we have, because we realize our own need as well as the need of the world. Maturing is needed—and required. Love is not a static thing, but something that is dynamic, ever changing, and growing.

Love is the evidence, or the fruit of the new birth, so if we are Christians it will show up in the good works we do toward mankind. When we love, others feel it, we feel it, and God is glorified. It's a win-win proposition.

QUESTIONS FOR DISCUSSION

1. How do you define love?
2. How do Christians love the unlovely?
3. Are there things we can do to make love grow?
4. What is the correlation between love and a holy life?

Mind Your Own Business

I Thessalonians 4:11–12 *Make it your ambition to lead a quiet life, to mind your own business and to work with your hands, just as we told you, so that your daily life may win the respect of outsiders and so that you will not be dependent on anybody.*

There are two ideas about witnessing that need to be considered: 1) witnessing with our words, and 2) being a living witness. Both are good and are needed, but one is more natural and effective.

Here we see Paul's prescription for the method of being a witness. First, he says to lead a quiet life, but that doesn't mean to lead a dull existence. It means to obtain a tranquil spirit of peace and a humble attitude. This is done by taking oneself off the throne.

There are some practical applications involved in leading such a life. Paul tells the members of Christ's church that it is important to mind our own business. In other words, it's necessary for God's children to try and stay out of trouble, especially when some folks seem to find trouble even when they are not looking for it.

Everyone should be cautious about sticking our noses in where they don't belong, but especially the disciples of Jesus need to learn the importance of recognizing and following the leading of the Lord before involving themselves in the affairs of others. Instead of meddling where we don't belong, we should learn to work with our own hands and be productive in a society filled with laziness. The goal for the follower of Christ is to be a rock that can be depended upon instead of being a sponge that just takes from every source it can. The bottom line is for Christians to be consistent over the long haul, because the Lord doesn't need His church to have the instability of ocean waves.

As a bonus then the believers could see the result of being a witness. By acting in this way, they could win the respect of outsiders by destroying an incorrect stereotype of the Christian faith. One can only wonder how many people are seeing the wrong image of Christ from people who call themselves Christians, but then take advantage of others. The church needs to present a correct picture of our Lord, for it is the only Christ that many will ever see. Opportunities to express such a witness for Christ can be opened if we ask the Lord to provide the vision for the harvest and then look with eyes of faith to find opportunities to be used by God for His glory.

When this kind of witnessing comes into play, one learns the meaning of independence, spiritually and physically, and we can be free to be dependent on God. So, don't just do witnessing; be a witness.

QUESTIONS FOR DISCUSSION

1. Is Paul's guidance about living a quiet life still possible in our ultra-busy world?
2. How does "quiet living" impact our being a witness for Christ?
3. Can one be a leader without being a follower also?
4. What do you think is the most effective way to witness for Jesus?

The Sleep of Death

I Thessalonians 4:13 *Brothers we do not want you to be ignorant about those who fall asleep, or to grieve like the rest of men, who have no hope.*

Death is a mystery to all of us, but we need to try and imagine the world in Paul's day. The Christians were under persecution from the Jews, misunderstood by the Greeks, betrayed by family and friends, suffering worse than the heathen world, and were often tempted to go back to their pagan lives. In such a situation Paul's message comes ringing through loud and clear to the people of God. He did not want them to be uninformed.

When he speaks of those who fall asleep, he is referring to those who have died. People then and people now continually are curious as to what happens to those who close their eyes for the last time and their hearts stop beating. Is this life all there is? Is there a world beyond this world? What happens to the body that is left behind? Will we be ghost-like spirits for all eternity? These and many more questions come from those who walk in faith with Christ and those who don't. Can we have answers to these questions on this side of the grave?

The answer to that last question is "yes" and "no." There are some things that we will not know until we cross over and receive the destiny that God has laid out for us, but there are some things we can know. First, we don't have to grieve like people who have no hope.

I have conducted hundreds of funerals and memorial services over the years of my ministry and there are some things common in them all. There is a sense of loss because regardless of the deceased person's faith status, those who love them will miss having them around. Sometimes there is a sense of relief because the departed one had been in severe suffering for an extended time, or the ravages of dementia or Alzheimer's disease had taken its toll. Sometimes saints rejoice over the promotion status of the child of God who has been called heavenward, and sometimes people grieve deeply because all visible evidence seems to show that the person was not ready to meet God.

What we can know about those who depart this world is that they will meet a God who never makes a mistake. Whether guilty or guiltless, the Maker of all things will know the truth beyond a shadow of a doubt and each person will receive what they deserve based on how they lived their life here. God is merciful and He is just. No one will get into heaven by the skin of their teeth.

This is why we have hope. Faith in Christ wins the victory—always.

QUESTIONS FOR DISCUSSION

1. Can you share something that has brought grief to your life?
2. Is death, particularly our own death, a source of grief?
3. Is there such a real thing as good grief?
4. How can ministry evolve from a situation of grief?

The Coming of the Lord

> **I Thessalonians 4:14–16** *We believe that Jesus died and rose again and so we believe that God will bring with Jesus those who have fallen asleep in him. According to the Lord's own word, we tell you that we who are still alive, who are left till the coming of the Lord, will certainly not precede those who have fallen asleep. For the Lord himself will come down from heaven, with a loud command, with the voice of the archangel and with the trumpet call of God and the dead in Christ will rise first.*

Okay, there is a lot to digest here, so we need to unpack it carefully. We need to understand that Paul is presenting the belief package of the church concerning what will happen at the end of the age, and within this package there are some basic tenets for us to hold on to.

First, it needs to be understood that we believe Jesus really did die and came back to life in power on the third day after His death. We celebrate that fact every Sunday and especially each year when Easter rolls around. Second, we believe that though Jesus went to be with the Father in the heavenly realms, He is going to someday bodily return to this world. Third, when His return happens, it will not be a secret, for there will be no vanishing of bodies from this world in a "rapture" type scenario. There will be a loud command, the trumpet of God will sound, and "At that time the Son of Man will appear in the sky, and all the nations of the earth will mourn. They will see the Son of Man coming on the clouds of the sky, with power and great glory" (Matthew 24:30). "Look, he is coming with the clouds, and every eye will see him, even those who pierced him; and all the peoples of the earth will mourn because of him. So shall it be! Amen" (Revelation 1:7).

We also believe that when Jesus comes, all those who have died in the faith will return with Him to establish His Kingdom on the newly transformed earth. At that point the bodies of the returning saints will be raised and transformed into their eternal forms, like the resurrected body of Jesus, and their spirits that have been in heaven will be reunited with their eternally resurrected bodies. They will live forever in God's beautiful redeemed creation.

After the dead have been reunited with their glorified bodies, then those who are still alive on this planet will be likewise transformed into their eternal forms and they too will live forever in the paradise of God. Paul relates in I Corinthians 15:51–52 "Listen, I tell you a mystery: We will not all sleep, but we will all be changed—in a flash, in the twinkling of an eye, at the last trumpet. For the trumpet will sound, the dead will be raised imperishable, and we will be changed." Thanks be to God! Amen!

QUESTIONS FOR DISCUSSION

1. What is the present status of those who have "fallen asleep," or died?
2. Does this scripture negate the concept of a "rapture" of believers?
3. How does the death and resurrection of Jesus speak to the idea of the future state of Christians?
4. When Jesus comes again, will everyone see Him?

Going to Meet the Lord

I Thessalonians 4:17–18 *After that, we who are still alive and are left will be caught up together with them in the clouds to meet the Lord in the air. And so we will be with the Lord forever. Therefore encourage each other with these words.*

In Paul's day, when a Roman leader would have a military victory and would return from his conquest to the gates of Rome, the whole city would turn out to meet them outside the city gates and then usher in the triumphant warriors with great fanfare. They didn't go out and stay out, but brought in the victors to enjoy the spoils of victory within the confines of home.

That's what Paul was talking about in these verses. He was not saying that people who are alive at the second coming of Christ will leave this world behind and go on to spend eternity in heaven, but that they will meet their Lord and usher him into His new Kingdom, the new earth. Revelation 21:1–4 makes this clear:

Then I saw a new heaven and a new earth, for the first heaven and the first earth had passed away, and there was no longer any sea. I saw the Holy City, the new Jerusalem coming down out of heaven from God, prepared as a bride beautifully dressed for her husband. And I heard a loud voice from the throne saying, "Now the dwelling of God is with men, and he will live with them. They will be his people, and God himself will be with them and be their God. He will wipe away every tear from their eyes. There will be no more death or mourning or crying or pain, for the old order of things has passed away.

The following verses of Revelation chapters 21–22 describe in more detail the events to come, but our focus is back to what Paul is saying to the people in the church at Thessalonica. Let me summarize what the apostle tells us:

This world has no hold on the people of God. Jesus has given us our freedom from the world because the church is going to be meeting Him face to face someday.

This world has no hope like the people of God. Those who have no hope are ignorant of the facts—and the promise. Those who have no hope are doomed to experience fear and grief, but the Church of Jesus Christ knows a very different story and a very different ending.

This world has no home like the people of God. We are promised to be with Him forever in a redeemed world. Even so, come, Lord Jesus!

QUESTIONS FOR DISCUSSION

1. Who will be alive when the Lord returns?
2. What does it mean to "meet the Lord in the air?"
3. Does this scripture bring joy or fear to us?
4. When we are with the Lord forever, where will that be?

CHAPTER FIVE

Times and Dates

I Thessalonians 5:1–3 *Now, brothers, about times and dates we do not need to write to you, for you know very well that the day of the Lord will come like a thief in the night. While people are saying, "Peace and safety," destruction will come on them suddenly, as labor pains on a pregnant woman, and they will not escape.*

Man has always dealt with the questions about the unfairness of life. The wicked are promoted, the righteous suffer, the good die, and the bad live. But the Day of the Lord will be a day of setting accounts, for it will be the end of the world as we know it, the last judgment at the second coming of Christ.

How does one prepare for such a time? Paul proposes three ways. First, we are to be knowledgeable of the facts. There is so much speculation concerning the topic of the end times that it's often confusing for the average Christian, but here are some basic truths we can count on.

Fact # 1 – Jesus is coming back. The Bible and our faith are based upon that promise. We have been informed and none of us can plead ignorance. In fact, we can sense His coming if we are His, and as we read through passages like I Corinthians 15 and Revelation 21, our excitement about this promise should fill us with joy.

Fact # 2 – He will come when few expect Him. "Like a thief in the night," is the phrase Paul uses. The Pharisees wanted a sign from Jesus and even Jesus' own disciples wanted to know the future from Him, but the only signs we will receive are those of Noah (Matthew 24:37–39) and Jonah (Matthew 12:39–41). The sign of Noah is that things will carry on like they always have, and the sign of Jonah is the preaching of repentance. The stage is set for the coming of the King of kings.

Fact # 3 – It is our responsibility to be ready for Him. Every person will appear before God and every person will stand alone before Him. Nobody's faith, except our own, will count at that point. According to worldpopulationreview.com, around the world in 2023, 166,324 people will die each day. That's 6,930 deaths per hour, or 116 deaths per minute, or 1.93 deaths per second. One thing that we know for sure is that death has been a reality for all mankind since the beginning of time, and no one has come back from it to never die again—except Jesus.

People deny, scoff, and ridicule the idea of our Lord's return, but their opinions will not change these facts in the least. God will have the last word and when He says that time is up, time is up—and no one will change that fact.

QUESTIONS FOR DISCUSSION

1. What is your understanding of "the day of the Lord?"
2. In what other context is the term *"thief in the night"* used in the Bible?
3. Was Paul making a comment about his own time with the concept of impending destruction, or about some future time?
4. How would you explain the return of Jesus to people who are ignorant of the biblical presentation?

Sons of the Light

I Thessalonians 5:4–7 *But you, brothers, are not in darkness so that this day should surprise you like a thief. You are all sons of the light and sons of the day. We do not belong to the night or to the darkness. So then, let us not be like others who are asleep, but let us be alert and self-controlled. For those who get drunk, get drunk at night.*

Not only does Paul advise believers to be knowledgeable of the facts, but he also tells them to be aware of their standing. There are only two groups possible in his thinking: Group one—those belonging to the night, and Group two—those belonging to the day.

The group belonging to the night is described in two ways: Those who sleep or have careless indifference concerning spiritual disciplines (which today could include church attendance, financial stewardship, personal and family welfare, etc.). Jesus calls all who will follow Him to a life of total commitment; to a life of holiness. Paul also describes this group as those who get drunk (or have irresponsible behavior). This is the crowd who abuse the grace of God—those who are defiantly selfish and sinful.

Then we have group two—those belonging to the day. These people are alert and watching. They are like a hostess watching for visitors, a teenager waiting for a birthday party or a card from someone special, or children who are waiting for Christmas. There is a sense of excited anticipation in their countenance. The truth of the matter is that Jesus is coming back. Are we watching for Him? We are only if we are self-controlled. Therefore, it's a matter of arming ourselves and realizing there is an ethical connection to being "in the light."

How we see God's grace is very much like Paul's description here. There are those who appreciate this wonderful gift from God and dedicate their lives to showing their gratitude by how they talk, act, and live toward those around them, and in spiritual devotion. These are people of the light. On the other hand, there are those who take God's grace for granted and assume that because God is so loving, He would never do anything that would cause them grief. They count on the fact that they have fulfilled spiritual rituals like baptism, taking communion, giving offerings, and attending worship services. Beyond those things they live like people of darkness, never considering that God expects more than lip service. Of course, there are those who totally ignore or reject the things of God on every level. Both groups are included as being in the darkness.

In Ephesian 5:8 Paul would say, "For you were once in darkness, but now you are light in the Lord. Live as children of light." May it be so.

QUESTIONS FOR DISCUSSION

1. Do the ideas of light and darkness depict and spiritual dualism, or could something else be possible? What?
2. How are people of the darkness described?
3. How are people of the light described?
4. How do Christ best live as the children of light?

Preparing for Battle

I Thessalonians 5:8–11 *But since we belong to the day, let us be self-controlled, putting on faith and love as a breastplate, and the hope of salvation as a helmet. For God did not appoint us to suffer wrath but to receive salvation through our Lord Jesus Christ. He died for us so that, whether we are awake or asleep, we may live together with him. Therefore encourage one another and build each other up, just as in fact you are doing.*

Along with the advice from Paul to be knowledgeable of the facts, and aware of their standing, the third admonition is to be encouraged in the Lord. How does the thought "the Day of the Lord," affect you? Do we fully realize that it is not God's will that we should die, but that we should live and be saved (John 3:16–17)? We sometimes distort the Old Testament image of God by not grasping what He intended for us to understand. He is not just a God of wrath, though His justice will be perfect and firm. The "Day of the Lord" is meant to bring the people of God comfort. We receive salvation through Jesus Christ, for He died for us so that we could rest in Him. We are the Lord's here—and hereafter. Therefore, we are to comfort and encourage each other with these thoughts.

Notice how Paul uses the weaponry of his day to depict the weaponry of the Kingdom. The breastplate, a shield used for defense in battle, is replaced with faith and love. The helmet, which is also used for defense in battle, is replaced with the hope of salvation. These words are not used accidentally. We are secure in the Lord by obtaining the faith, love, and hope that He has provided for us. We don't have to worry about how this world treats us, or even physical death, because the presence of the Holy Spirit never leaves us, and we are always in the care of the Almighty.

Salvation cannot be overemphasized. We who put our trust in Jesus for life and life everlasting, have received something more precious than gold and more durable than diamonds. We who have been sealed with the seal of God means He knows who is His own. We don't have to worry about the enemy being greater than our Lord, or of us not being able to complete our mission for the Master. God has appointed us and God has predestined us to receive salvation through His Son. It doesn't mean that we don't have a choice, but it does mean that God wants us to be saved more than anything. He has worked out His plan for us to perfection and He wants us to realize just how much He loves all His creation.

For people to not take advantage of God's great offer of life is the ultimate act of stupidity and selfishness. Jesus died so we don't have to. Thanks be to God for His priceless gift of life eternal!

QUESTIONS FOR DISCUSSION

1. Does Paul's of metaphors like the "breastplate" and the "helmet" help in understanding what he is trying to say or not?
2. Does the Day of the Lord excite you or frighten you?
3. Can you explain what it means to be with Christ whether we are awake or asleep?
4. What are some good ways for us to encourage one another in the faith?

The God-Called Leaders

I Thessalonians 5:12–13 *Now we ask you, brothers, to respect those who work hard among you, who are over you in the Lord and who admonish you. Hold them in the highest regard in love because of their work. Live in peace with each other.*

It's important that we understand that we should not advertise what we cannot produce. The world needs to see holiness "where the rubber meets the road" because holiness is more than an ivory tower doctrine; it is an overhauling of our lives to move us from selfish to selfless. Jesus is coming for us and in light of this fact we need a holy life to be found pleasing to Him, so Paul helps us to find emphasis in the right areas. This means we need a holy relationship with those who lead in the walk with God. We are to love and respect our spiritual leaders, realizing it is God's will for them to labor among us.

I have been blessed in relationships with good men of God who have helped shape my life in so many ways. There were the pastors that brought me into the faith as a child and guided my steps as a teenager, the lead pastors who served as my bosses when I was ministering with youth, music, or outreach, and the district superintendents that have governed my work as a lead pastor myself. I owe them much for their dedication to the work God called them into and for how they impacted my own ministry. Along with these men who were my mentors, I have been challenged by the younger men and women whom I have mentored along the way. Collectively, I am aware that these people of God have helped make me the person I am today, and I owe them all a great debt of thanks.

Paul wasn't out to get pats on his own back, but he was laying down a principle that needed to be passed along to all generations. When God sees fit to call a person into His service as a minister of the gospel, it is never something to take lightly. Every pastor ought to be reminded of the admonition from James, who said, "Not many of you should presume to be teachers, my brothers, because you know that we who teach will be judged more strictly" (3:1). That's the role of a God-called minister of the gospel, and he or she ought to be held in high esteem because of it.

With the passing of each generation there requires more young people who will stand up and answer the call of God to serve Him through the church. It's not an easy life and often a thankless one, but one that the world needs more and more. We should all pray that the Lord of the harvest will raise up more workers to serve Him. But if we have a pastor, we need to lift that person up to God in prayer and give thanks for such a blessing that God gives to a congregation.

QUESTIONS FOR DISCUSSION

1. Who has been the person that was your strongest example of walking with Christ?
2. In what ways can we show respect for those who preceded us in the walk of faith?
3. When we are admonished by people of faith, does it cause discouragement or encouragement?
4. Can we learn anything from the advice Paul gives here?

Being Accountable

I Thessalonians 5:14–15 *And we urge you, brothers, warn those who are idle, encourage the timid, help the weak, be patient with everyone. Make sure that nobody pays back wrong for wrong, but always try to be kind to each other and to everyone else.*

Accountability is required of a pastor and accountability is required of the laity. One may be willing, able, and ready to train another in some line of work, but the trainee must be willing to be trained. The same is true for the body of Christ, for no one grows without wanting to do so.

It's God's will for Christian leaders to be "over" the laity. As the old saying goes, too many chiefs or cooks can spoil the end result. Although there needs to be many advisors, there can only be one leader at the top without having confusion and disorganization. The pastor is looking at things from a different view. Therefore, it's not prudent to go against men or women of God—unless we have heard from God directly in the matter. It's God's will for us to be at peace with them because there should be peace among the body of Christ if there is peace anywhere.

We also need a holy relationship with those who trail in the walk with God. We all see signs of "drifting" now and then, and therefore we are to provide a warning ministry for those who won't do what they are supposed to do, and for those who do what they are not supposed to do. We are to warn them out of our own past experience and out of a heart of love.

What this means is that we are to provide an encouraging ministry. Literally, this is for those with "small souls." It means tender treatment for tender hearts, and it means we provide courage through our example. We are also to provide a strengthening ministry, caring enough to evangelize, to disciple, and enough to bind them to the church. Finally, we are to provide an enduring ministry. We are not to give up on the ones who trail or are weak, because God hasn't given up on them, and someone didn't give up on us.

Paul concludes this section by emphasizing that we need a holy relationship with those who offend in the walk with God. We are not to pay back wrong with wrong. There isn't a place for revenge in the Christian's life. We are also to try to be kind to all because there is also no place for unkindness in the Christian walk. However, this is only possible through the fullness of Christ's Spirit of love.

Holiness is a matter of keeping up to date with Jesus. If we will, He will guide us in our relationship with others. If holiness doesn't affect our relationships in our dealing with all people, then the experience isn't real.

QUESTIONS FOR DISCUSSION

1. Is being idle a sin?
2. Do you think Paul words here apply to all believers, or just to those who are church leaders?
3. Why is revenge such a bad thing?
4. How can we hold people accountable to do what Paul is requiring?

This is God's Will for You

There aren't many scriptures that get more specific than these when it comes to determining God's will for your life. Earlier Paul had specifically said, "It is God's will that you should be sanctified..." (4:3). Sometimes it's hard to discern what God wants for our lives, but when we see it this clearly, we need to pay attention.

Basically, Paul was saying, "Be joyful! Nobody likes a sourpuss." Joy is a better witness than gloom. The more infrequently you see people, the more important it is to make your time with them count for Jesus.

Joy is not happiness. Happiness is something you can chase all your life, but you will never find it for long. It is fleeting. Joy is not put on, however, or worked up. It is within, given by God, or it is not at all.

He was also saying, "Be prayerful! The hotline is always open." Prayer is the key to making each occasion a blessing. Asking God to make every contact we have an opportunity is a good way to start the day. Prayer is the key to help us to focus on what's important. If we aren't concerned about something enough to pray, then we really aren't too concerned about it. Prayer is important in keeping your relationship with God intact, for how can you be in love with someone that you don't spend time with? How can we know more about God without centering on Him in prayer?

Finally, Paul wrote, "Be thankful! Remember who is in charge." Thanksgiving is not about my perception; it's about His providence. My vision is so very limited. I never really saw the United States until I lived outside its borders for a few years. We who live here have come to depend on certain things as entitlements and rights rather than privileges. But God's plan is vast and complex. Who can understand eternity? Who pretends to fully know the mind of God outside of the Bible?

Thanksgiving is not about my preferences; it's about His purposes. What I want is governed by my comfort zone. Blessings are often rated directly in proportion to how good they make me feel. God may want to bless me in ways that hurt for a time, and I need to be thankful even for these things.

Thanksgiving is not about my problems; it's about His presence. When we dwell on our problems, we stay unhappy and bitter. When we focus on His presence, we become overwhelmed by His blessings.

The key to these things is the fact that they are God's will for us as we abide in Jesus, so be joyful, pray, and give thanks!

QUESTIONS FOR DISCUSSION

1. Are the three commands of Paul here dependent on each other or is it possible to achieve one without the others?
2. Is it really possible to give thanks in all circumstances?
3. Why do you think that these things are God's will for us?
4. Do you think people are affected more by our joy or by our thanksgiving attitude?

Don't Quench the Spirit!

I Thessalonians 5:19–22 *Do not put out the Spirit's fire; do not treat prophecies with contempt. Test everything. Hold on to the good. Avoid every kind of evil.*

As the Apostle Paul closed out this letter, he had some specific instructions for the people of Thessalonica to remember. We could learn a lot from them too. The warning is to not put out the Spirit's fire.

Specifically, he said, "Do not make light of prophecies." There are two ways of looking at prophecies scripturally. There is "fore-telling," and the gospel of Matthew builds a good case for this with the repeated statement, "that it might be fulfilled," concerning many of the Old Testament proclamations that came true in the New Testament. However, there is also "forth-telling," and this is usually what Paul and others biblical writers meant, for prophecy in its purest sense is preaching. Both meanings are included in the Bible though and we want to take them both seriously, for we are not to be critical of things we don't fully know or understand.

He also said, "Don't believe everything that you hear." We are a society run amok with rumors—and the internet and social media only compound the problem. We are also amid a society of churches that have run amok with false doctrines and "half-truths." That's why Paul said we are to test and prove what is prophesied (or preached), for we will only be able to discern what is wrong if we know what is right. Otherwise, it's just our opinion against others. If it doesn't match the whole tenor and context of scripture, we are to leave it alone. We must remember that a text out of context is only a pretext, for the Bible can never say what the Bible never said.

One way for us to be effective in our study of God's Word is to put questions to our study. Going back to the lessons we learned in our early days of public schools where we asked, "who, what, where, when, and why," would be a good place to start. Who are the characters? Who was the writer writing to? What was the situation addressed by the writer? What was the writer's purpose in putting his words down in script. Where does the setting take place for the writing and receiving? When did it happen in history? Why did it make a difference when the writing was first received, and why should it matter to us today? If we would set apart the stories of the Bible and answer those simple questions thoroughly, we would be greatly ahead of the average churchman who just reads the Bible only. As the people of God, let's hold on to the good and let go of the bad. This is the surely the will of the Lord for His redeemed creation.

QUESTIONS FOR DISCUSSION

1. What does it mean for us to "put out the Spirit's fire?"
2. How can we know if prophecies are real or not?
3. What kind of tests are required for us to know truth from falsehood?
4. How far do we have to go to avoid evil, like Paul says here?

Sanctified!

I Thessalonians 5:23–24 *May God himself, the God of peace, sanctify you through and through. May your whole spirit, soul, and body be kept blameless at the coming of our Lord Jesus Christ. The one who calls you is faithful and he will do it.*

Another instruction that Paul gave to this church was to not settle for just being saved (23). Being saved is a wonderful experience in the Lord, for it's both a crisis and a process. No one ever gets saved without the prevenient and redemptive grace of God, and we don't grow without continually changing. Being sanctified is being completely surrendered. It is part of the crisis and part of the process. Going on into entire sanctification is God's plan, and we need to realize that it is not an option for the Christian who really wants God's will to be fulfilled in his or her life. It's evidenced by the fruit of the Spirit at work in our lives and the death of the works of the flesh (Galatians 5:19–23). Blamelessness is not faultlessness, but it's the result of a complete submission to the work of God's Spirit in our lives that frees us from guilt and the penalty of the nature and work of sin.

For some, this whole idea of a second work of grace, is confusing. I like to clarify it like this: When a person comes to Jesus Christ and is saved, born again, redeemed, or whatever label one puts on it, he or she gets all of God there is. God doesn't hold Himself back from the person who genuinely seeks Him. However, when a person is sanctified wholly, God gets all of the seeker. Our submission to Him is complete and we are willing to do anything, go anywhere, or be anything He wants us to be. This is why it is important for the child of God to be saved and sanctified.

Paul continued the closing of this letter by telling the church, "Don't forget who does the work" (24). God is the One who inspires prophecies, for no true prophet ever proclaims on his or her own. God is the One who saves from sin. All the good works we will ever do will not take away our sins. God is the One who sanctifies the believer. He calls us to holiness, and He alone can make it possible. God is the One who keeps us in His care, for the One who sustains the universe can sustain our walk with Him.

Too many Christians try to live their walk of faith on their own. They may start off strong, but then the enemy comes to them and tries to defeat the good work that God has done in them. This is why we need to be fully saturated with the Holy Spirit of God and controlled by the grace that redeems us. We will never be strong enough, wise enough, talented enough, or gifted enough to defeat the enemy on our own. We need to be sanctified completely so that the battle can belong to the Lord!

QUESTIONS FOR DISCUSSION

1. Can you explain what Paul means by "sanctification?"
2. How can we be sanctified "through and through?"
3. What is the difference between being blameless and being faultless?
4. How will God do what need to be done in us?

- 49 -

Pray for Us

There was never a time when Paul didn't need the prayers of God's people to support his ministry efforts. He traveled widely and in his travels he continued to share the news of what Jesus Christ had brought to pass in our world, but as he did so he faced many difficulties as a result. He didn't go into detail here, but merely asked for prayer. As he did so, however, he set a precedent that we need to consider for our daily walk with the Lord.

Each Sunday when the church gathers, it needs to have a time when the body of Christ can pray for each other. We need to lift up the work of our ministers, whether clergy or laity, to the Lord as they each take up their respective tasks in society. In some parts of the world there is liberty to share Christ freely, but in well over half the nations there are some kinds of legal restrictions as to whether or not Jesus can be shared. Some allow it in only private settings, and some don't allow it at all. Still, that doesn't change the Great Commission given to us by Jesus. It just means that some may face greater tribulation than others because of their political and social environments.

It especially behooves the family of believers to pray for those who are continually in the work of church planting and for those who are in harm's way. We are not only to pray for our own, but for peace in our society, peace from war, and peace in our homes. God is always pleased when there is harmony among His creation.

Paul felt that it was important that this letter would be shared widely among the fellowship of believers. Obviously, the recipients did just that, for we are still reading it today. God's Word continues to be translated into many world languages and dialects so that the scriptures can become a love language of the heart for many nations.

Finally, he says, "Do not forget each other." They were not only to pray for each other, and love each other as they shared God's Word with each other, but they were to enjoy the grace of Christ together. Few things are more beneficial to the church than fellowship among its people. There are enough conflicts heaped upon believers by the world, so in the times we have together we need to express support and compassion toward each other as much as possible. We are to have an open ear, an open mind, and an open heart. If we will do that, then God will do the rest.

QUESTIONS FOR DISCUSSION

1. When we get a general request for prayer, like this one, how do we respond to it?
2. Is a "holy kiss" something we should continue to do in our churches?
3. What impact do you think a letter like this had on the Thessalonian Church?
4. Is the pronouncement of "grace" just a benediction, or do you think Paul meant something more from it?

INTRODUCTION TO SECOND THESSALONIANS

II Thessalonians

The Apostle Paul, along with his coworkers in the gospel, Silas and Timothy, wrote a second letter to the church that was established in Thessalonica on Paul's second missionary journey, as recorded in Acts 17. Most early church fathers agree, including Clement of Alexandria, Tertullian, and Irenaeus—dating back to the year A.D. 200, on the authorship of Paul. However, there have been some who have doubted that Paul was the author on the grounds that the writer's view of eschatology (study of last things) differs somewhat from Paul's other letters. It has been suggested that a follower of Paul's may have written this letter using Paul's name (a practice that was commonly done in the first century). Some have even suggested that Silas was the author and that it was written after Paul's death, which would place the writing around A.D. 75. There is no hard evidence for this view, however, so we will consider for our purposes that Paul was indeed the author of this epistle.

Thessalonica, which was the capital and largest city of the Roman province of Macedonia, served as a center of trade and commerce. This made the city vitally important to Paul and to the cause of Christ. A strong church was established there despite a rough beginning and multiple persecutions. It was mainly a Gentile church and its membership included men named Jason (Acts 17:9), Aristarchus, and Secundus (Acts 20:4).

From all appearances, it would seem that this second letter was written within a year of the first, possibly within a few months. That means the letter would have been written from the same location as the first, in Corinth, sometime around A.D. 50-52 (Acts 18:1-11).

Paul was encouraged by the news brought to him by Silas and Timothy about the progress and standing of the church. He wrote the first letter to express his joy that had been raised, and he challenged the church to holy living, as in keeping with the cause of Christ.

Apparently, some message had come to Paul following the reception of the first letter. The second letter was sent to the church to further encourage it during days of persecution, but also to correct some misconceptions concerning the second coming of Christ. It also imparted the role of discipline for members who didn't live up to the standard that Paul, in Christ, had set for them.

CHAPTER ONE

Greetings to the Saints

II Thessalonians 1:1–2 *Paul, to the church of the Thessalonians in God our Father and the Lord Jesus Christ: Grace and peace to you from God the Father and the Lord Jesus Christ.*

Here we find the members of the team who are traveling on Paul's second missionary journey. It's the same trio that Paul listed in his first letter to this church (I Thessalonians 1:1). Paul was the leader and prominent church planter. Silas was originally sent out with Paul and Barnabas by the church council in Jerusalem (Acts 15:22) to share the council's rulings concerning the Gentile church. He became the replacement companion for Barnabas, who left Paul when the two of them had a disagreement over whether Barnabas' nephew, John Mark, would be allowed to go with them on this second journey. John Mark began the first missionary tour with them (Acts 13:5), but abruptly returned home in the midst of the work (Acts 13:13). It seems that Paul lost confidence, patience, or both with him because he apparently deserted the team.

In any case, Paul at this point traveled with Silas, and along the way they picked up Timothy (Acts 16:1), a young man whom Paul took into his heart as a co-laborer in his gospel spreading endeavor. Timothy became Paul's "true son in the faith (I Timothy 1:2), and though an apprentice at this point, he would eventually become the bishop of Ephesus and a key figure in the developing church of the first century.

The church at Thessalonica was planted by Paul earlier on this second missionary journey amid conflict and a very brief stay—only three weeks (Acts 17:1–10). From this reference in Acts we find that the church was initially made up of several Jews, some God-fearing Greeks, and several prominent women of the community, but some time had passed by the writing of this letter from Paul. We don't have a lot of other historical information, but from his first letter it appears the church was faring well (I Thessalonians 3:6–8).

From this introduction Paul thought the church to be a faithful part of the Christian family, for they were "in God and Christ."

Verse two provides a common greeting for Paul. Every letter he wrote to the churches began in a similar way, and though it is true that grace and peace are no small matters, his desire that this church and all the others should receive these blessings from God is no secret. Sometimes he added the word "joy" to the mix or changed the words around some, but basically Paul was just writing a greeting that was customary for him.

QUESTIONS FOR DISCUSSION

1. How do you think the Thessalonian Church benefited from receiving these letters from Paul?
2. Have you ever given thought to writing encouraging letters to distant churches, say in another country even?
3. Why was it important for Paul to address this letter from both God the Father and the Lord Jesus Christ?
4. Do you consider the Paul's mentioning of "grace" and "peace" as just a greeting, or could these words mean something more?

A Reason to Give Thanks

II Thessalonians 1:3–4 *We ought always to thank God for you, brothers, and rightly so, because your faith is growing more and more, and the love every one of you has for each other is increasing. Therefore, among God's churches we boast about your perseverance and faith in all the persecutions and trials you are enduring.*

One thing that excited Paul was the fact that the faith of this baby church was growing. Nothing brings more joy to a parent than to see his or her child doing well, and that is just what Paul was feeling. The author of Third John echoed that sentiment when he wrote, "I have no greater joy than to hear that my children are walking in the truth" (vs. 4). However, when it comes to the matter of obtaining a growing faith, it must be realized that this can only happen when one's faith is being tested. We may wish that easy times would make us strong, but that doesn't seem to be the case.

The church at Thessalonica was being tested greatly. First, Paul was attacked and likewise his followers suffered for the sake of the gospel of Christ. The words of Jesus ring true for all generations, "A student is not above his teacher, nor a servant above his master" (Matthew 10:24). If those we follow are persecuted, this it is likely that we will be also. Such was the case of Paul and the followers of Christ in this church.

The difference here, however, is that Paul gave God thanks for this. As iron sharpens iron, so adversity sharpens the church, and the apostle knew that at the end of the testing these baby Christians would shine like their Master and Lord. We should always give God praise for the times we are in pressured situations because such is the Kingdom of God, for we are all in the process of being made like gold. Eighteen hundred years ago, the church father, Tertullian, said, "The blood of the martyrs is the seed of the church." Some things never seem to change.

Paul was also grateful that their brotherly love was increasing. Love is seen through service to others, and the more one serves the more one grows. What begins as duty often becomes a great joy. How wonderful is the love of God when it begins to wear off on those whom He has touched.

Finally, Paul said that he was thankful that the endurance of these believers was so great that it was worthy of his boasting. This is not because they were bearing hardship passively, but because they were enduring and overcoming victoriously. For all these things, the apostle offered up thanksgiving to God—and we should do the same ourselves.

QUESTIONS FOR DISCUSSION

1. What are some indications that this church is doing well?
2. What causes faith to grow?
3. Is it right for Christians to boast when things are going well?
4. How does the fact that the church was experiencing persecutions and trials speak to the issue of the current "Health and Wealth Gospel" message?

Worthy Before the Lord

II Thessalonians 1:5 *All this is evidence that God's judgment is right, and as a result you will be counted worthy of the kingdom of God, for which you are suffering.*

The one thing we can always count on is that God is always right. The suffering that people endure for righteousness' sake will be counted as worthy by God. In other words, God honors those who honor Him and especially those who face hardships for putting Him first.

It's good to know that even as sure as we have human frailties, missteps, and sometimes poor judgment, God doesn't suffer from any of these things. His wisdom cannot be overstated. Paul would elaborate on this in Romans 11:33, "Oh, the depth of the riches of the wisdom and knowledge of God! How unsearchable his judgments, and his paths beyond tracing out."

Most of the time most of us don't feel very worthy. We all know people who are smarter, more talented, richer, better looking, and have much more to offer the Lord. In fact, we usually wonder about the amazing grace of God that would even offer life with Him forever to us. Who are we that we should claim the highest privilege of being God's child?

Paul tells us here that God is the highest judge of such matters and He says that when we suffer for His sake, we are considered worthy in His eyes of being citizens in the Kingdom of God. We just can't do any better than that.

I have witnessed others who have suffered for Jesus, but I have not been asked to be in that number at this time. It may come, and I pray that if it does, I will be willing and able to stand firm for Christ in the time of such testing. The most I have ever had to face was some snarky comments and perhaps some eye-rolls from unbelieving connections, but I want to always be able to put Jesus first, regardless of the cost.

In Revelation 6:9–11, the saints of God who had been martyred for the faith, waited at the altar of God for these deaths to be avenged. They were told to wait until the total number of martyrs would be reached, but they were then told that the Lord would act. We may not understand such a scene, but of course, we are told that the Lord is aways right.

The day may come when we will suffer for the Lord, but if it happens, let's do it with joy. Such experiences make us worthy in God's eyes.

QUESTIONS FOR DISCUSSION

1. Is God at work, judging us at this present time?
2. How is one counted worthy before God?
3. Can you explain what Paul means about "the kingdom of God?"
4. Is it better for us to suffer for the kingdom than to not suffer?

The Justice of God

II Thessalonians 1:6–8 *God is just: He will pay back trouble to those who trouble you and give relief to you who are troubled, and to us as well. This will happen when the Lord Jesus is revealed from heaven in blazing fire with his powerful angels. He will punish those who do not know God and do not obey the gospel of our Lord Jesus.*

God has a way of balancing the scales of justice for the promise here is that the troublemakers will be troubled by God, and He will provide relief to the deserving.

We can also be sure that Jesus will come from heaven in due time with great power to bring about judgment. He will punish those who have rejected God and don't live up to the words of the gospel.

In the same way we know that God is always right, we know that God is always just. He will never contradict His written Word and He will never tempt people to do things that are evil. Because we have all been given a degree of insight just from the natural creation around us, we all will stand before Him someday and give an account as to what we did with the knowledge He has revealed to us. Romans 1:18–20 emphasizes this very fact:

The wrath of God is being revealed from heaven against all the godlessness and wickedness of men who suppress the truth by their wickedness, since what may be known about God is plain to them. For since the creation of the world God's invisible qualities—his eternal power and divine nature—have been clearly seen, being understood from what has been made, so that men are without excuse.

People around us often live as if they will live forever without penalty, or they live as if God doesn't see what is really going on. Thankfully, we have the Bible to give us instructions for holy living and what it really means to please God. God will always have a people, but not all dogs go to heaven (to steal from a movie title), and not all people do either. There will be a day of reckoning where perfect justice will be administered and those who deserve God's wrath will receive just that.

Paul didn't write this to discourage people, but to encourage the church, for their labors and endurance was not in vain. Ours isn't either, and as we trust in the Lord, we can expect the best He has to offer.

QUESTIONS FOR DISCUSSION

1. Is God's payback the same thing as karma?
2. Do you think that Paul expected Christians to experience trouble?
3. How will Jesus be revealed to us?
4. Will punishment be the same for those who don't know God as those who know but don't obey?

Preaching the Gospel of God's Son

II Thessalonians 1:9–10 *God, whom I serve with my whole heart in preaching the gospel of his Son, is my witness how constantly I remember you in my prayers at all times; and I pray that now at last by God's will the way may be opened for me to come to you.*

As I consider these words, I have now passed the fiftieth anniversary of my first sermon. It was on March 18, 1973 when I was asked to bring a Sunday evening message in a small Michigan community during my days in college. It was a night I will never forget. There was a twenty-three-inch snowfall on the ground with drifts that rose to the house tops and barn roofs. Some people came to worship on snowmobiles.

I bombed big-time! The whole sermon was only about seven minutes long and I literally shook as I stood before that massive audience of about fifteen people. It wasn't God's power that was shaking me, but nervous stage fright—for I was a terribly shy teenager and I had much to overcome.

Still, God never gave up on me and eventually I got the courage to try again. Throughout the years since that frigid evening, what happened to Paul happened to me. I devoted my whole heart to the preaching of the gospel of God's Son and I have never regretted the call that was divinely placed on my life. God's power not only transforms sinners, but He emboldens and encourages preachers to keep after the mission to which He has assigned them.

A call to preach the gospel of Jesus Christ is also a call to pray. Paul prayed for this congregation and prayed that he could be reunited to them so that they all could share together in the blessings of the Lord. The same is true for every believer, for we all stand in need of God's grace to help us along our journey in life, as well as to lift up each other. There is no way that we are ever going to be able to make it alone. The Christian walk is not through will power, mind over matter determination, or an emotional zeal that gives us the victory. We rise or fall through our connection to Christ or lack of it, and that truth is the same for every generation.

A whole-hearted ministry produces fruit that will glorify the Master. Though we may or may not receive a salary for our work in the Kingdom of God, there is no such thing as part-time service for the Lord. For as long as we have breath, we have an assignment. So whether we preach, pray, travel, or stay put, we are on commission from the Lord, and as long as that is the case, we've got plenty to do.

QUESTIONS FOR DISCUSSION

1. Can one serve God without serving Him with one's whole heart?
2. What is the Gospel of Jesus Christ?
3. How is it possible to pray at all times?
4. How can we know that something we pray for is God's will?

A Purpose in Prayer

II Thessalonians 1:11–12 *With this in mind, we constantly pray for you, that our God may count you worthy of his calling, and that by his power he may fulfill every good purpose of yours and every act prompted by your faith. We pray this so that the name of our Lord Jesus may be glorified in you, and you in him, according to the grace of our God and the Lord Jesus Christ.*

Here Paul gives a reminder of his constant prayer support for this baby church. He basically prayed three things for them. First, he prayed that the believers would live up to what they were called to do.

Every Christian has a purpose and so does every local church. Oftentimes, a mission statement is made up by a group of believers, for it helps us to always keep our focus on the main thing that Jesus has called us to do. That will vary according the spiritual gifts of the individual churchmen and the collective gifts of the worshiping body, but God knows how to equip people to fulfill His purpose for each of us where He plants us.

The second thing Paul prayed for was that God's power would strengthen them in all they attempted to accomplish through faith. It cannot be said enough that God's power is at the source of all we ever accomplish for good in this world. By faith we take on the mission God has given us, and then we rely on power from on high to do in us and through us all that needs to be completed.

The final thing Paul prayed for in these verses is that Christ would be glorified in the midst of His people. For this church and for every church, there needs to be a purposeful, concentrated effort in all of our worship services to bring glory to the name of the Lord. It can be done through the songs we sing and play, the focus we put on God's Word, or the fellowship that we enjoy together because of His love that binds us. We also glorify Him when we leave our public gatherings and go off to our individual tasks of the week. At that point we become Christ to our world as we allow His Spirit to make Himself known through our words, attitudes, and actions. Whether together or alone, we are called to bring glory to the King.

Paul made it clear that the Thessalonian church and the worldwide church today is not alone. It never was and never will be. One of its main tasks, however, is to keep the main thing the main thing. If that can be done, then the rest will take care of itself under the care of Almighty God.

QUESTIONS FOR DISCUSSION

1. Are we living up to what God has called us to do?
2. Are we to act if not prompted by faith to do so?
3. How can we make sure Christ is glorified when we come together as His church?
4. How is the grace of Christ applied to our services when we come together?

CHAPTER TWO

Anchored in Reality

II Thessalonians 2:1–2 *Concerning the coming of our Lord Jesus Christ and our being gathered to him, we ask you, brothers, not to become easily unsettled or alarmed by some prophecy, report or letter supposed to have come from us, saying that the day of the Lord has already come.*

This is one of the more difficult passages to interpret in all of the New Testament because of the time and cultural differences that we have from when it was first written. The ideas Paul was writing about were common to his readers in the first century, but seem distant and strange to us.

He was basically saying here that Christians have to get over their emotional, irrational ideas about the second coming of Christ. Our faith in the ultimate plan of God is to be what anchors us, not what unhinges us. In essence, Paul was saying that believers are not to be troubled concerning the coming of Jesus. It is to be a glad day for the faithful, for that is what we as people of faith look forward to. But it will be a fearful day for the lost who have not put their faith in Christ as Lord and Redeemer.

He also said that the believers were not to be troubled by false proclamations that come in the form of prophecies, rumors, or even through writings. In Paul's day as well as ours, there were those who would focus on the spectacular and mysterious rather than on the actual Word of God. There must have been some people who were circulating letters in Paul's name, and he wanted people to know that such false information should not be listened to or followed. Such things may cause concern for the unenlightened, but the apostle tried to steer this young congregation away from sensational doomsday proclamations. They were not to be troubled over information that was false.

In our own time there are many well-meaning people who forward information on the internet that often does not have any base in fact. Just because someone said something, wrote something, or reported rumors of something that supposedly has happened or will happen, is not reason for

Christians to give up their ability to reason or to focus on going to God as our Divine Source for our daily truth.

God doesn't want people to check their brains at the entrance of the sanctuary. Jesus warned us to be wise as serpents, but harmless as doves (Matthew 10:16). That means we need to trust the Holy Spirit to guide us, but not to be influenced by the words of men alone.

QUESTIONS FOR DISCUSSION

1. How would you explain the return of Jesus to someone who doesn't understand it?
2. What does our being "gathered to him" mean?
3. What is the "Day of the Lord?"
4. Why should believers be at ease when it comes to thinking about the end times?

"That Day!"

II Thessalonians 2:3–4 *Don't let anyone deceive you in any way, for that day will not come, until the rebellion occurs and the man of lawlessness is revealed, the man doomed to destruction. He will oppose and will exalt himself over everything that is called God or is worshiped, so that he sets himself up in God's temple, proclaiming himself to be God.*

Specifically, the apostle was saying that the believers should not be deceived in two particular areas. First, they should not be deceived about recognizing the Day of the Lord. When Jesus comes again, everyone will know about it. Check out the following verses:

At that time the sign of the Son of Man will appear in the sky, and all the nations of the earth will mourn. They will see the Son of Man coming on the clouds of the sky, with power and great glory (Matthew 24:30).

For the Lord himself will come down from heaven, with a loud command, with the voice of the archangel and with the trumpet call of God, and the dead in Christ shall rise first (I Thessalonians 4:16).

He will come without any previous warning, but all will see Him.

> *But the day of the Lord will come like a thief. The heavens will disappear with a roar; the elements will be destroyed by fire, and the earth and everything in it will be laid bare* (II Peter 3:10).

They were also instructed not to be deceived by the man of lawlessness. So, who is this man? There are as many opinions about his identity as there are people to offer them. Some believe Paul was talking about Nero and the power of Rome, which would eventually attack the church and take Paul's life. Others see this person to be in the line of papal succession, while still others hold that it is someone who is yet to come on the scene, but will do so shortly before the second coming of Christ.

All we know for sure is what we read in the Bible, and contained in it are some brief glimpses of truth concerning this man. First, we see that he is the author of rebellion. Second, we see that he opposes all that is holy. Third, we note that he tries to take the place of God in a worship setting and proclaims himself to be the highest spiritual authority. Beyond these brief descriptions of him we are really left to wonder and speculate. What Paul was trying to say directly to the church in Thessalonica may or may not apply to us today, for some things may have to remain a mystery.

QUESTIONS FOR DISCUSSION

1. Does it matter if we don't know who the "man of lawlessness is?"
2. What attributes does this "man of lawlessness" possess?
3. Does not knowing the future bother you?
4. How can we best be prepared for whatever comes?

The Power of Lawlessness

II **Thessalonians 2:5–7** *Don't you remember that when I was with you I used to tell you these things? And now you know what is holding him back so that he may be revealed at the proper time. For the secret power of lawlessness* *is already at work; but the one who now holds it back will continue to do so till he is taken out of the way.*

It is this part of Paul's letter to the Thessalonians that cause some New Testament scholars to question whether these are actually the words of Paul. The whole idea of the "man of lawlessness," is not found in any other of his writings and they produce a different eschatological (last things) view from other specific passages, like I Corinthians 15.

Some say that this evil personage is the "Anti-Christ," and those who espouse a "rapture" theology testify that his appearing will come after the rapture of the church has taken place. However, there is much debate concerning the reality of a church rapture, particularly from me, since I find that the idea of the church being taken out of the world is found nowhere in scripture, I believe there must be another explanation.

We must always keep in mind the old adage that though the Bible was written for us, it was not written to us. This letter was not given first-hand to the church of the twenty-first century, but to the local church in Thessalonica nearly 2000 years ago. What Paul related to the church of his time had to make sense to them, even if it is confusing to us. When these words were written the temple in Jerusalem had not yet been destroyed, so it is probable that Paul was taking imagery from the book of Daniel concerning the "abomination of desolation" (Daniel 12:11) that Jesus also mentioned (Matthew 24:15).

Whichever way one interprets Paul's words, it is clear that in his day this event of evil was still in the future, but was being held back by the purposes of God. The evil one already had an influence in the ancient world though, and probably was what John was referring to when he wrote: "Dear children, this is the last hour; and as you have heard that the antichrist is coming, even now many antichrists have come. This is how we know it is the last hour" (I John 2:18).

Much of what we need to understand these verses remains unknown to us. There are many opinions to be viewed and this format doesn't allow us to look at them all. But next we will take another look at the words given to us and trust God to help us understand what we need to know.

QUESTIONS FOR DISCUSSION

1. Is the man of lawlessness someone about whom we should be concerned?
2. What would you surmise the "secret power of lawlessness" to be?
3. How should Christians today approach the idea of "Anti-Christ?"
4. What is the Christian's secret power to be an overcomer?

Lawlessness and Satan

II Thessalonians 2:8–10 *And then the lawless one will be revealed, whom the Lord Jesus will overthrow with the breath of his mouth and destroy by the splendor of his coming. The coming of the lawless one will be in accordance with the work of Satan displayed in all kinds of counterfeit miracles, signs and wonders, and in every sort of evil that deceives those who are perishing. They are perishing because they refused to love the truth and so be saved.*

Though the lawless one that was described by Paul here has a great following because of the travesty of evil that he displays, he will be revealed for what he is by the Lord at the proper time. God has the timeline of eternity all planned out and we can rest assured that nothing or no one is going to slip something by Him.

There are a couple of things to notice from these verses. First, whatever the evil one is up to, it is going to be undone by the power of Jesus. When He comes again, the work of the devil and his minions will be destroyed and we will be free from the influence of evil forever. We can give thanks to God for that!

A second thing that catches my attention though, is that those who follow after this person who is a tool of Satan, will be destroyed as well. Though the gospel is free and anyone can take part in the life of salvation that is offered, the sad truth is that not everyone will. Many will continue in their sinful ways until they reach the end of their journey in life, and they will pay for their rebellion and disobedience just like this lawless one. There will be those who will believe the lies of the evil one and their reward will be to reside with him.

Jesus made this clear when He was preaching, for He said:

Enter through the narrow gate. For wide is the gate and broad
is the road that leads to destruction, and many enter through
it. But small is the gate and narrow the road that leads to life,
and only a few find it (Matthew 7:13–14).

This is a hard passage, but we can count on some solid truths from these words. First, there is a genuine and real force of evil in the world, and secondly, God is in ultimate control and neither evil, nor the evil one, is any threat to Him or His authority. He will have the last word and will triumph completely at the end of the day.

QUESTIONS FOR DISCUSSION

1. How will the "breath" of Jesus' mouth and the "splendor of His coming" overcome and destroy the lawless one?
2. What are the works of Satan that deceive those who are perishing?
3. Why are the perishing, perishing?
4. Do you think that the "lawless one" is literal or is this a metaphor?

The Great Lie and the Great Liar

II Thessalonians 2:11–12 *For this reason God sends them a powerful delusion so that they will believe the lie and so that all will be condemned who have not believed the truth but have delighted in wickedness.*

Jesus warned His disciples that they should be aware that the enemy of their souls would be trying to trick them in the days to come. If there is one thing that is consistent about the devil, it is that he continually lies. When speaking about the Jews who challenged Him, He said: "You belong to your father, the devil, and you want to carry out your father's desire. He was a murderer from the beginning, not holding to the truth, for there is no truth in him. When he lies, he speaks his native language, for he is a liar and the father of lies" (John 8:47).

That's pretty clear. Jesus also warned people about the deception that would abound concerning His second coming. "At that time if anyone says to you, 'Look, here is the Christ!' or 'There he is!' do not believe it. For false

Christs and false prophets will appear and perform great signs and miracles to deceive even the elect—if that were possible" (Matthew 24:23–24).

When people who should know better, continue to walk contrary to the light the Lord gives them, that light will eventually be taken away as mankind experiences God's wrath: "The wrath of God is being revealed from heaven against all the godlessness and wickedness of men who suppress the truth by their wickedness, since what may be known about God is plain to them, because God has made it plain to them" (Romans 1:18).

Once individuals make the deliberate choice to leave the things of God behind, they are engulfed in darkness. After living in such a blind state for a period of time it becomes impossible for them to move back into the light and return to God. That is, it's impossible for man, but not for God. He is able to reach through the fog and bring the unbelieving back into the faith even when none of us can find the way on our own. However, no one is guaranteed such an offer when God's grace has been rejected. Darkness drags us into deeper darkness if we are left to our own devices.

Society is filled with false gods, miracles-working sooth-sayers, and spiritual hucksters. The sleight of hand from the devil works wonders on many who fall victim to his lies. Let us walk in the light of the Lord so that we can overcome and help others to overcome as well.

QUESTIONS FOR DISCUSSION

1. Do you feel that God is really the source of delusion?
2. Does God cause people to believe lies?
3. Are some people condemned by God from the start?
4. How wicked does a person have to be in order to "delight" in it?

Lots of Reasons to Give Thanks

II Thessalonians 2:13–14 *But we ought always to thank God for you, brothers loved by the Lord, because from the beginning God chose you to be saved through the sanctifying work of the Spirit and through belief in the truth. He called you to this through our gospel, that you might share in the glory of our Lord Jesus Christ.*

Paul always seemed to have something for which to be grateful. He didn't see the churches under his charge as a cross he had to bear, but rather as a joy that blessed his ministry. We could learn something from his attitude.

He said that we ought to be thankful that God chose us. In one sense it is true that we are predestined, for God chose us from the beginning. This is not our beginning, but the beginning of His plan for the world. We are not just an afterthought with God, for He has plans for each of us and He has the big picture with the smallest details and contingencies worked out.

God chose us to be saved. Just think and imagine the circumstances that brought about your salvation. It was not an accident, for this is God's prevenient grace—the grace that goes before we even knew about Him—to bring us into His Kingdom. We are being saved through the sanctifying work of the Holy Spirit, which is a process that takes place over time, but also at a crisis moment when our full surrender has been made and God cleanses our hearts from all things that would keep Christ from being the true Lord of our lives.

He chose us to be called. We are saved for a purpose. We are saved to serve God through the acts of serving others. We are the ones who have been made aware of our rescue and know what we were rescued from. As we believe and are justified by Christ, we are then given a task to do. Too often too many have not yet come to this truth.

He also chose us to share in the glory of the Lord Jesus Christ. It's a pretty good benefit plan that He has in store for us. We only have a little taste of it down here, but Paul elsewhere wrote of the deposit the Lord has provided for us: "Having believed, you were marked with a seal, the promised Holy Spirit, who is a deposit guaranteeing our inheritance until the redemption of those who are God's possession—to the praise of his glory" (Ephesians 1:13b–14).

There is no doubt about it—life is good, but the best is yet to come!

QUESTIONS FOR DISCUSSION

1. Who is it who causes you to give thanks to God for them?
2. What is the "sanctifying work of the Spirit?"
3. Does God choose only some to be saved?
4. How can we share in the glory of Jesus?

Hold On to the Blessing

II Thessalonians 2:15–17 *So then, brothers, stand firm and hold to the teachings we passed on to you, whether by word of mouth or by letter. May our Lord Jesus Christ himself and God our Father, who loved us and by his grace gave us eternal encouragement and good hope, encourage your hearts and strengthen you in every good deed and word.*

Paul calls the church to be faithful. "So then," is the result of God's choice for us, or God's predetermined plan, for us to inherit salvation. We are told to "stand firm" and to "hold" to what we were taught. We stand firm knowing that it is not a call to live as those who were saved, sanctified, and petrified, and it is not a call to boycott change, or a call to remain ignorant and ineffective. Standing firm is keeping faith with what God considers to be important. We dare not get caught up in the games of man to the point that we lose sight of God's big picture of reaching the world with the message of holiness.

The admonition is given to "hold" to what we have been taught. It's a call to remember what we have heard. The preaching of the Word helps us to become saturated and based in the truth of God, and causes us to stay focused on the Great Commission that was given to us by Jesus.

God wants us to be blessed, and He wants us to live lives of blessing. Paul said that this can occur through two avenues. First, this happens through God's encouragement in our hearts. Paul already knew God's love and God's support of his own ministry and he already had hope through God's work in his life. He was saying that it is now time for the new Christians in Thessalonica to get in on the truth and the blessings. God builds us up as we draw nearer to Him.

We can also be blessed through God's strength in our words and actions. If we will deliberately focus our thoughts on the Lord, then our hearts will be encouraged. If we deliberately focus our thoughts on the Lord, He will help us to reflect Him to others in what we say and what we do. This is the only pathway to peace. It's also the only way outsiders can see that we as Christians are different from those who are not in Christ.

Attitude is not just some little thing in the Christian life; it's a huge thing! It's our witness of what God has done and is doing in us through Christ.

A thankful spirit, a consistent walk, and an example of a life that has been blessed will not only make us stronger, but will glorify the God who has saved us. Our witness of Him makes Him look good—and that's our goal!

QUESTIONS FOR DISCUSSION

1. How do we "stand firm" in the Lord?
2. What encourages your heart in the faith?
3. How are you strengthened in the faith?
4. What part do good words and deeds play in our spiritual growth?

CHAPTER THREE

How to Pray

II Thessalonians 3:1–2 *Finally, brothers, pray for us that the message of the Lord may spread rapidly and be honored, just as it was with you. And pray that we may be delivered from wicked and evil men, for not everyone has faith.*

We often think of the Apostle Paul as the great prayer warrior who interceded for the many churches that he planted throughout his ministry. While this was no doubt a true description of him, he was also a man who himself was in need of prayer as much as anyone else. This passage shows us a great man who was not too proud to see that he needed the body of Christ to carry him in prayer, just as he had often prayed for others.

This passage teaches us a lesson in how we can learn to pray for our spiritual leaders. Here we learn what we should pray for. First, we should pray that the message they preach will spread rapidly. For any of us, there is only so much time to work, and people only have so much time to receive the message of eternal life. If a person finds Christ at eighty years of age, a soul has been saved. But if a person finds Christ as their Savior at age eight, then a life has been saved as well. The clock measuring our humanity is ticking for all of us, and certainly a valid prayer is that those who are spreading the good news of Christ and those who are receiving the good news of Christ, will be successful in the matters of delivery and reception.

Second, Paul taught us to pray that the message will be honored. There is a veil of darkness blocking people from receiving the gospel message. Jesus spoke of this in His parable of the Sower in Matthew 13:18–23; Mark 4:15-19; and Luke 8:12-14. The gospel cannot be honored until the veil is removed, and it is removed as people are broken before the Lord.

In Luke 2:23–25, when Jesus was taken to Jerusalem as a baby, there was a man named Simeon, who was an elder among the people of Israel. Because of his faithfulness, God had promised him that he would not die until his eyes would behold the Messiah of redemption. When addressing Mary, he said,

"This child is destined to cause the falling and rising of many in Israel, and to be a sign that will be spoken again." His words were prophetic for people of all generations, because no one ever rises until they first have fallen. There must be a humbling of self before one can lift up his or her head to serve the Lord. God has a way of breaking us before He can use us for our good and His glory.

QUESTIONS FOR DISCUSSION

1. When you pray, what do you pray most about?
2. How regular are your prayers for the propagation of the gospel?
3. Do you pray for your own personal safety?
4. How do people "get" faith?

More Lessons About Prayer

II Thessalonians 3:1–2 (continued) *Finally, brothers, pray for us that the message of the Lord may spread rapidly and be honored, just as it was with you. And pray that we may be delivered from wicked and evil men, for not everyone has faith.*

A third idea to consider is that not only is there a prayer request here for the message going forth, but also a prayer for the safety of those who would carry it. Paul acknowledged that not everyone would be receptive to the message God has released through Christ, and evil men abound who would do everything in their power to stop its truth.

We often are sheltered from such attacks from these evil men, but there are many Christians down through the centuries, and even now, who have paid, and are paying the ultimate price to share their faith. Thousands still die, and according to estimates of various international commissions, more than 200 million people in over sixty nations are presently being denied their basic human rights for one reason only—because they are Christians.

Paul also prayed for deliverance from faithless men. Many are not anti-Christ, but are just numb to the claims of our faith. Apathy, not antagonism, is the greatest threat to the church in the United States, Europe, and in many parts of the Western world. Too many churches are filled with passionless people, and the apostle acknowledged this as a threat to the cause of Christ.

One of the greatest weapons that we will ever have is the power of prayer.

Prayer puts us in contact with the throne of God through the avenue of His Holy Spirit, and once we have touched the presence of God we can be assured that unlimited resources are available to us.

There will always be wicked men and women until the Kingdom of God comes in its fullness. Though the devil is a defeated foe, he is doing all he can in the time that is left to him to take as many people down with him as possible. Mankind is God's highest creation and our enemy's highest goal is to destroy what God loves most.

Therefore, we are to join with Paul and pray for the Lord's message to be spread and honored, and for the saints who carry the message to be protected from harm as they do the work of God. Around the world the Kingdom is growing and prayer links us all together in the Lord's name.

QUESTIONS FOR DISCUSSION

1. What can we do to help spread the gospel rapidly?
2. What is our obligation to the Christians who are living in harm's way?
3. How does prayer bring about our protection?
4. Does the gospel require persecution of believers in order for the unbelievers to be brought to faith?

Why We Should Pray

II Thessalonians 3:3 *But the Lord is faithful, and he will strengthen and protect you from the evil one.*

Not only did Paul remind us "what" we should pray for, but also gave us the reason as to "why" we should pray. We should pray because the Lord is faithful. Nothing that men can do will ever change His attitude toward us or all mankind. We also need to remember that nothing God will ever do will be done out of any other motive but love for us.

Here is where we should ask the same question of our own lives. Are the things that we do motivated and moved by love? How Christlike are we? A check-up on this very important point is warranted in our lives from time to time.

We should pray because the Lord will strengthen us. We are strengthened by our coming together as His body on earth.

What then shall we say, brothers? When you come together, everyone has a hymn, a word of instruction, a revelation, a tongue or an interpretation. All of these must be done for the strengthening of the church (I Corinthians 14:26).

We are strengthened out of God's vast resources and we are strengthened by remembering His promises to us.

Now to him who is able to do immeasurably more than all we ask or imagine, according to his power that is at work within us, to him be glory in the church and in Christ Jesus throughout all generations, for ever and ever! Amen (Ephesians 3:20–21).

We should also pray because the Lord will protect us. If we live and endure, He is with us. If we die and go on to glory, we are with Him. It's a win-win situation for the Christian. This may explain Paul's words in Philippians 1:21–24:

For to me, to live is Christ and to die is gain. If I am to go on living in the body, this will mean fruitful labor for me. Yet what shall I choose? I do not know! I am torn between the two: I desire to depart and be with Christ, which is better by far; but it is more necessary for you that I remain in the body.

Either way, to live or die, a Christian cannot lose! We are on the winning team for all eternity through our Lord Jesus Christ.

QUESTIONS FOR DISCUSSION

1. Can you name three ways that the Lord has been faithful to you?
2. How has the Lord strengthened you?
3. How has the Lord protected you?
4. How do we shield ourselves from the "evil one?"

The Results from Prayer

> **II Thessalonians 3:4–5** *We have confidence in the Lord that you are doing and will continue to do the things we command. May the Lord direct your hearts into God's love and Christ's perseverance.*

From these verses we learn what happens because of prayer. Prayer produces confidence, for the more one sees what prayer does, the more faith is increased. The more one has faith, the more one prays.

Pray also produces obedience. When you know you have a meeting each day with someone who knows your schedule intimately, it affects how you run your schedule.

Prayer produces accomplishments because prayer moves the hand of God. The Bible is full of examples as to how God responded to the prayers of His people. He certainly hasn't changed, so we today can count on Him to answer our prayers as well.

Prayer produces growing hearts of love because prayer is also about relationship building. When we bring someone before the Lord, we get to know them better. It's impossible to earnestly pray for God's best for others without drawing closer to them with our own hearts.

Finally, prayer produces perseverance. It has been said that it takes twenty-one days to develop a habit. It therefore takes perseverance to continue in prayer, but the discipline of doing so brings about grace to continue in our walk with the Lord.

The goal that is above every goal for the Christian is to glorify God. We are to present Him in such a light that others will see Him for who He truly is and be drawn to Him in love and devotion. That will only happen if we live our lives in such a way that people will see God at work in us and want what we have.

The Apostle Paul was concerned about this matter in regard to the church in Thessalonica. Rumors were coming to him that Christians were not setting Christ-like examples of industry, but instead some had become lazy or idle. No doubt many felt that since Jesus was going to return soon that there was just not much of a reason to work, since all would soon be gone anyway. Paul had some admonishing words to say to set the record straight for this church and all churches. We will deal with this tomorrow, but until then, we need to stay at our posts and be the best we can be for the sake of our witness to the world about our King!

QUESTIONS FOR DISCUSSION

1. What does it mean to "have confidence in the Lord?"
2. How important is our "doing" in order to maintain our "being?"
3. How can we know if the Lord is directing our hearts?
4. What is Christ's perseverance?

The Authority of "the Name"

II Thessalonians 3:6 *In the name of the Lord Jesus Christ, we command you, brothers, to keep away from every brother who is idle and does not live according to the teaching you received from us.*

Paul had a strong concern for authority. He knew that without an authoritative foundation any society is adrift, and if that is true for the world then how much truer it is for the church. He calls upon "the name," for the name of Jesus is the highest authority on any subject. The unbelieving world will malign the name, but Christians revere the name of Jesus above every other authoritative source. We who lead households of faith must take great pains to be sure that our families understand this.

It is much easier to say such things in the 21st century than to actually live them out. Perhaps in days gone by, when the church was the only activity in town for social events, it was easier to be more loyal to the things of Christ, but those days are for the most part long gone. In most communities with a western-culture there are so many things calling for the right to be the authoritative source, that it is difficult for many, as the old hymn says, to keep "holiness unto the Lord" as their "watchword and song." A myriad of sports programs for children, teenagers, and adults head the list, followed by a company of many legitimate distractions like work, charity service, community projects, and social entertainments, that cause the Christ of Christianity to be shoved to the back-burner, or to be ignored altogether.

There was a time when no Christian would work on the Lord's Day, for it was set aside for rest and worship, and only the jobs that demanded attention to prevent loss of life or prevent suffering were excluded. Today, restaurants and department stores have their busiest days on Sundays and church groups have often changed from having evening worship services to going bowling, skating, or partying in the name of reaching the youth or becoming "all things to all people."

Certainly, it was Jesus who said, "the Sabbath was made for man and not man for the Sabbath" (Mark 2:27), but one wonders if He would even recognize the church in the form it has often become. From the pulpits of the world there are often sermons concerning self-help, self-esteem, and self-advancement through the process of developing a healthy self-image, but not as often does one hear about self-denial, self-sacrifice, or self-abasement. Maybe for God's sake it's time to re-evaluate these things.

QUESTIONS FOR DISCUSSION

1. What authority does Paul have to list his commands as "In the name of the Lord Jesus?"
2. Are there qualifications to what idle Christians other believers should avoid?
3. If one doesn't live according to the teachings of scripture, are they to be considered Christians?
4. What are the basic requirements to be a Christian?

A Command Against Idleness

II Thessalonians 3:6 (continued) *In the name of the Lord Jesus Christ, we command you, brothers, to keep away from every brother who is idle and does not live according to the teaching you received from us.*

Whatever we give our time, money, and devotion to is our authoritative source and our god, whether it is football, income, entertainment, or Christ. Paul emphasized that "the name of the Lord" is to be revered and honored. What we say and do as Christians needs to make God look good, or glorified.

It is in this context that Paul gives a command against idleness. This is not a request or a subject for debate, so he gave a strong prescription to address this problem as it was being experienced by the Thessalonian family, and that command was for spiritual isolation. He said to stay away from every idle "brother." It was the church that was being judged here, not the world. The church never has the right to judge the world, for that responsibility belongs to God alone, but it is the church's responsibility to judge itself—and that includes all who profess the name of Christ. In this situation Paul had already judged and had set the discipline required to be that of ostracism. Those who were faithful were to have nothing to do with those who were being lazy until there was a lifestyle change from idleness to productivity. It was a prescription meant to bring awareness of the problem, and hopefully repentance and restoration. Paul didn't boot people out just to be mean, but that they might be restored. For that reason, he said that when Christian people don't live according to the doctrine he had handed down, the church was to treat them as strangers and stay away from them.

We sometimes take it lightly, but correct doctrine is one of the most important features of a church. Every pastor and Christian leader should take his or her responsibility in this matter very seriously. It's not usually a fun job, but it is essential for the body of Christ to be kept pure before the Lord who created it.

The world's media is continually looking for a juicy story of people in the Christian community who have fallen from their place of leadership. There is no shortage of people who are more than happy to point their accusing fingers at the church for any kind of slippage from the holy ideal. Therefore, we need to take care to show a true picture of Jesus to the world in all we do and say so that the Father will be glorified, not scorned.

QUESTIONS FOR DISCUSSION

1. What would you consider to be idle behavior in the 21st century?
2. Is there a biblical age for retirement in the Christian faith?
3. Does the command to "keep away from every brother who is idle," mean excommunication from the fellowship of believers?
4. Is this command to exclude people from the fellowship of believers to be temporary or permanent?

Standing Against the Tide of Greed

II Thessalonians 3:7–10 *For you yourselves know how you ought to follow our example. We were not idle when we were with you, nor did we eat anyone's food without paying for it. On the contrary, we worked night and day, laboring and toiling so that we would not be a burden to any of you. We did this not because we do not have the right to such help, but in order to make ourselves a model for you to follow. For even when we were with you, we gave you this rule: "If a man will not work, he shall not eat."*

Paul gave us an example of how to live. He was not idle; in fact, there have been few men who have been more ambitious than Paul. He did not eat without paying for it and not because it was a rule he had to live by, but it was a principle that he chose to uphold so that he would not be a burden. No doubt there would have been an easier way for him to make a living, but he didn't want anyone to doubt his sincerity or his motives. He most likely preached and taught the gospel through the day and worked on his tent-making at night. However, he did it because he considered his duties more important than his rights. As the leader of the church, he could have taken a salary or support from the various congregations that he started, but he chose a different course.

He set down a standard for the church to follow, "If a man will not work, he shall not eat." This again, is a principle that must be administered with wisdom. There are extenuating circumstances that may cause a man to be unable to work, but rather than being a fast rule for this concept of industry, it is a principle and guide for Christians to follow.

What a contrast Paul's actions and attitudes are to the standard practice of many in our twenty-first century Western society. There are now generations of people in the United States who have learned how to "work the system" and are milking the government, the church, and anyone else they can tap, just to get money without working. This has nothing to do with thievery, although that clearly is listed among the sins Paul describes from time to time. This speaks of plain laziness and societal greed that is just as corrupting.

From the Lottery to the Welfare state, too many people are gaming the system either in the hopes of getting rich quick or forcing others to pay for their laziness through government programs. Charity is one thing, but when it is abused, it stops being of God. Christians need to learn the difference and like Jesus, learn to give instead of taking.

QUESTIONS FOR DISCUSSION

1. What kind of example are you setting for other believers to follow?
2. Are Christians to not receive charity?
3. Is it a correct practice for Christian pastors to be paid by the body of believers, or should they work outside the church for their income?
4. How far do we take the admonition, "If a man will not work, he shall not eat?"

Not Busybodies, but Busy Bodies

II Thessalonians 3:11–13 *We hear that some among you are idle. They are not busy; they are busybodies. Such people we command and urge in the Lord Jesus Christ to settle down and earn the bread they eat. And as for you, brothers, never tire of doing what is right.*

The apostle dealt with rumors as they were relayed to him. The busybodies needed to get busy and be "busy bodies." They needed to learn to provide for themselves not only so they would be able to provide the necessities for their families and others, but particularly because lazy Christians are a bad reflection on Christ.

There are many social programs that were started from pure motives that have morphed into something that has become destructive. In the United States, the Social Security program was begun during the Great Depression in the 1930's in order to provide older Americans with a financial base to fall back on when they could no longer work. What began as a 3% tax of a worker's wages deducted to be held in escrow by the government for those rainy days, has now increased to the point that by law an employer must withhold 6.2% on the first $160,200 (up to a maximum tax of $9232.40), plus 1.45% Medicare tax for the first $200,000 of a worker's income, plus 2.35% Medicare tax on all employee's wages in excess of $200,000. This 7.65% of one's income withheld must then be matched by another 7.65% by the employee, reaching a total of a 15.3% reduction from a worker's paycheck before any other federal, state, and local taxes are taken out. The destructive part of this financial plan is that too many people have become solely dependent on receiving rather than working, to make sure that they are not just takers, but givers as well.

The taxing rate has changed drastically since it was first initiated however, but the point here is not to be a lesson in economics. It is to show how important it is for everyone to carry his or her fair share of the load to support each other. If older citizens are to be provided for, then there must be younger workers who are contributing to the retirement fund to make sure there is enough money in it to cover all benefits previously earned and promised. If there is not enough money saved to cover the expenses promised, then we have a breakdown in society's safety net.

This principle is the same in the Christian church. We are not to be lazy and be concerned only for ourselves, but generous to as many as possible as we work to be a blessing rather than a burden. This is the Christian way.

QUESTIONS FOR DISCUSSION

1. How much is too much when it comes to charity?
2. When does charity reach the point of dependent making?
3. Should the church stick to preaching the gospel or include social programs?
4. Is it wrong to refuse charity when it is offered in good faith?

Tough Love

II Thessalonians 3:14–15 *If anyone does not obey our instruction in this letter, take special note of him. Do not associate with him, in order that he may feel ashamed. Yet do not regard him as an enemy, but warn him as a brother.*

Paul believed that violators of his instructions needed to be disciplined, so his word went out to isolate the guilty ones in order that he or she would be ashamed of their actions. Again, Paul gave this command not to bring permanent separation, but for an ultimate healing in the body that would come about when the wayward person was restored. Brothers need to be admonished, not excommunicated, for we are all in this walk with Christ together for the glory of God. Our job is not to trim down the flock, but to build up the church and make it stronger than when we found it.

This is hard for us to do because the natural desire within us is to want revenge, or at least to extract justice from those who disregard the way that Jesus wants us to walk. It's really hard on two levels. First, we hate to have to discipline anyone because we want to always be loving in the hope that the disobedient will see the error of their ways and straighten up their act. Shunning them seems like an extreme measure to those who genuinely grieve for our backslidden brothers and sisters. The second reason this is hard is because when we are betrayed, trust is hard to regain. Even if those who wander away from the fold do change their ways and come back to faith, evaluating their sincerity is a challenge for the best intended disciple of Jesus.

When I struggle to find answers to my questions in the New Testament, I often try to find solutions from the Old Testament. One passage that caught my attention was Hosea 4:17, which reads, "Ephraim is joined to idols; leave him alone." In this instance, Israel was accused of adultery against God and though the Lord wanted to establish a solid relationship with His people, they were joined to idols. Therefore, God said through the Prophet Hosea that they were to be left to their foolishness and to face the judgment they had earned.

We know that God loves everyone. The Bible is full of examples to this fact, but we also know that He will not be trifled with. Paul knew this to be true, so he warned the church not to coddle those who chose to be unfaithful. Either they heed the gospel or they will face the One who is their Judge. We must always love, but sometimes tough love is needed.

QUESTIONS FOR DISCUSSION

1. Is it possible to evaluate a person's actions without being their judge?
2. How do we reach those with whom we don't associate?
3. Does isolation produce shame or just obstinance and anger?
4. Can we consider someone a brother that we ban from our connection?

Final Words

II Thessalonians 3:16–18 *Now may the Lord of peace himself give you peace at all times and in every way. The Lord be with all of you. I, Paul, write this greeting in my own hand, which is the distinguishing mark in all my letters. This is how I write. The grace of our Lord Jesus Christ be with you all.*

Here Paul bids the church farewell. He blessed them and prayed peace for them from the Author of Peace. He reminded them of the presence of Jesus who would be with them, and the grace that came from heaven alone. As he closed, he provided them evidence of his authority. Though he usually wrote with the help of a scribe—and there is some thought that this may have been because of his poor eyesight, possibly stemming from the bright light experience on the Damascus Road—he signed each letter to authenticate his words. Paul wrote to a church that was doing well, but needed to do even better. Though for having only a three-week foundation of training, they seem to have come a long way.

This letter shows that the church in Thessalonica had questions, and that Paul did his best to provide answers. By doing so he set down a pattern for superintendents and leaders of churches for all time. A brief summary of the contents of this letter shows that Paul emphasized four basic themes.

1. Jesus is coming again. Paul didn't know when the big event would happen and we don't either. We only know that God always keeps His promises and so we can expect Christ's return when the time is right. Just as the scripture says, "You see, at just the right time, when we were still powerless, Christ died for the ungodly." (Romans 5:6), we know that His return is in accordance with the perfect time as well.

2. Stand firm in your faith until He does return. Over and over Paul stressed the need for patience in our devotion to Jesus. We are in a marathon, not a sprint.

3. Be faithful and diligent in all your labors. Don't despair. God will reward the faithful in due time. Until that time we need to keep on keeping on.

4. Don't quit until you are relieved by the Master. He has not forgotten His own, for He promised to be with us until the end of the age.

These things are not bad advice for the church of any age.

Printed in the United States
by Baker & Taylor Publisher Services